CAVES OF ADVENTURE

CAVES

OF

ADVENTURE

by
HAROUN TAZIEFF

TRANSLATED FROM THE FRENCH BY ALAN HODGE

ILLUSTRATED WITH PHOTOGRAPHS

HARPER & BROTHERS

NEW YORK

CAVES OF ADVENTURE

Contents

Members of the Expeditions to the Caves of Pierre Saint-Martin

Two expeditions explored the Lépineux caves under the direction of Max Cosyns. The one in August, 1951, was composed of the following:

Max COSYNS	Robert-J. LÉVI
Jacques ERTAUD	Marcel LOUBENS
Jean JANSSENS	Giuseppe OCCHIALINI
Jacques LABEYRIE	Léon PÉROT
André LAISSE	PETITJEAN
Georges LÉPINEUX	Haroun TAZIEFF

The second expedition, in August, 1952, comprised:

Max COSYNS	Pierre LOUIS
Jean JANSSENS	André MAIREY
Jacques LABEYRIE	André MORIZOT
André LAISSE	Giuseppe OCCHIALINI
Robert-J. LÉVI	Jacques THÉODOR
Marcel LOUBENS	André TREUTHARD
Haroun TAZIEFF	

Preface

FIVE YEARS ago in the little limestone massif, or mountain mass, of Arbas, in the department of Haute-Garonne,
the exploration of a particularly difficult cave came to an
end. It was the cave of Henne-Morte, and for several
years it was to be the deepest yet discovered in France.
I mention it in this preface because it was Marcel Loubens's principal objective when he was making his debut
as a speleologist. And it was there that I met him.

In 1940 he explored the first shaft with Josette
Segouffin. In 1943 he and one of his companions were
injured, and it was a near miracle that Casteret and
Delteil managed to bring them out alive from a depth
of more than 650 feet. In 1947, sponsored by the Speleo
Club of Paris with the help of the army, the tenth expedition to Henne-Morte was finally successful. It gave
great pleasure to Loubens, who reached the bottom
of the cave at a depth of 1,463 feet. The wall beside the
underground river, which disappears into an impenetrable siphon, forever bears his name.

Henceforth, Loubens was bitten, as he put it, by the
"speleological bug," and he devoted every moment he

9

could spare to underground exploration. After Henne-Morte he sought in his native Pyrenees for another objective on the same scale; this was the beginning of his collaboration with Cosyns, who had long been attracted by the valley of Licq where the torrents converge that issue from the wonderful gorges of Holçarté and Kakouetta.

Great hopes were raised by Lépineux's discovery of the entrance to the caves now known by the name of Pierre Saint-Martin.* The first perpendicular drop is truly formidable—some 1,000 feet. It is tempting to penetrate thus into the heart of a mountain where the rumbling of powerful underground streams can be heard. But the lure of exploring the unknown is reinforced by practical interests, for it is a question of finding a flow of water, high above the level of the valley, that could be a source of generating power. The expedition of 1951 revealed the huge possibilities of the cavern and also the presence of an underground river.

Nevertheless, the work involved is heavy, especially for the men on the winch at the top; they have to exert a tremendous effort in order to haul men and their equipment, often weighing more than 200 pounds, up a

* Near frontier-stone 262, called Pierre Saint-Martin, there are several entrances to caves; the one with which this book is concerned ought more exactly to be called the Lépineux cave.

perpendicular stretch of 350 yards. Out of this difficulty came the idea of a winch with an electric motor, taking its current from a set of batteries. This solution, which was adopted, was certainly a good one, and probably the only one that could have allowed full latitude to the expedition. In face of the tragedy of Loubens's fall to death, however, one is forced to admit that the security precautions, which might have been good enough for an exploration on a lesser scale, were inadequate for a task involving such long and complicated maneuvers.

When he first took part in the exploration of the Pierre Saint-Martin caves in 1951, Haroun Tazieff was a newcomer to speleology. Hitherto, he had been distinguished as a volcano expert. He had toured the world as an alpinist and geologist, studying on the spot, from as close as he could get, the nature of volcanic eruptions. From the volcanoes of Africa, and from Etna and Stromboli, he had brought back evidence of the highest importance; his fine book, *Craters of Fire,** presents an impressive account of his activities and observations. In the caves of Pierre Saint-Martin, Tazieff was Loubens's companion. Anxious to explore the whole range of these underground caverns, like the rest of the team, he was ready for everything for the sake of the cause.

* To be published in the United States by Harper & Brothers.

Kewgee
Hamburg

Movingly, his book makes one live again through those tragic hours of 1952. Written with simplicity, and sometimes with a certain dryness that accentuates the extraordinary nature of the surroundings, Tazieff's volume sets the expedition against its true background and gives every member of it his full due.

This small group of explorers had undertaken a tremendous task, for it must be remembered that successful expeditions into the cavities of the earth require a very considerable deployment of men and equipment. Faced with the drama of Loubens's fall, the members of the expedition and their helpers displayed a magnificent team spirit. I am thinking of the scouts from Lyons, Louis and Georges Ballandraux, Daniel and Pierre Epelly, and Michel Letrone, who came up from another cavern in the neighborhood and rushed to lend their aid in the attempted rescue of Loubens. With equipment consisting only of ladders and ropes, these five young men, accompanied by Casteret, stationed themselves at intervals in the shaft to a depth of 790 feet. Clinging to their fragile ledges, they waited for a very long time in the huge perpendicular tube where any falling stone could become a murderous projectile.

I am also thinking of Dr. Mairey who went down to attend to Loubens, suspended from the same cable that had just given way beneath his friend's weight. The same Dr. Mairey and Tazieff, who were the last to remain at the bottom of the shaft, managed to find the courage and energy which made the expedition a real achievement. They would not come back to the surface until they had realized Loubens's project, which was to push the exploration to its end. In these tragic circumstances they made a most remarkable discovery: they found a huge magnificent cave, now named after Marcel Loubens, which opens into a vast gallery and leads to a large and swift-flowing underground river.

I would like to mention, as well, the efforts made on the surface after the accident. At the edge of the shaft, on the mountain, in the valley and far beyond, a host of men who have remained anonymous lent their strength without counting the cost.

What can one say now except to emphasize that all these efforts and sacrifices have not been in vain? Speleology has its casualties, and they are unfortunately all too numerous, especially when it is a matter of tackling long and deep subterranean caverns. But let us consider the aims of speleologists, whom the public at large are inclined to think of as sportsmen, only interested in breaking records. Sportsmen they certainly are, for physical strength, skill and adroitness are very necessary underground. They are also adventurers, like alpinists and discoverers of unknown places. But there is more to it than that. One is apt to forget that the speleologist's work can be extremely useful, both from the scientific and the practical points of view.

Limestone massifs cover an enormous surface of the globe, and in their recesses, caverns and galleries, many important underground rivers are concealed. At the moment we have knowledge of only a few of these cavities, but what we know adds up to an impressive total.

Generally speaking, limestone massifs are arid, and the waters they contain are subterranean, sometimes running at very great depth. It is of basic importance to understand where the waters originate, how they flow, where they come out and what ultimate connections they have with the springs and streams in the valleys. One could thus, for instance, trace the saturation area of a particular series of springs, and work out the possibilities of pollution and the measures of purification necessary to make the water drinkable. By drilling boreholes, one could also, for industrial and agricultural purposes, bring a river to the surface which would otherwise see the light of day only at a much lower altitude. Several boreholes of this sort have already been sunk—at Lez and Eaux Chaudes, for instance—and they produce falls of remarkable potential.

Besides these practical considerations, which are of immediate use to civilization, a wide range of physical and physicochemical research is possible, for the subterranean regions, more or less isolated from the world outside, are the scene of peculiar reactions and phenomena. In many other spheres, besides, the speleologist has a fruitful role to play. In geology, he supplies details on the thickness and the nature of the different levels traversed, and on ancient fillings that are evidence of higher strata long since washed away from the earth's surface by various forces of erosion and corrosion. In prehistory, he discovers magnificent underground museums containing works that were fashioned tens of thousands of years ago, and which express the sensibility, the artistic sense and the ritual tendencies of primitive man. These relics are nearly always far underground, and their discovery is often the result of descents down shafts, climbing exploits, diving and even adventurous subterranean canoeing.

In biology, underground exploration is the source of minute fauna belonging to innumerable species, the study of which has given rise to special laboratories and authoritative courses of instruction in the big scientific institutes. These tiny cave-dwelling creatures are really the greatest lords on earth, for they can trace their pedigree back to ancestors that have now disappeared and whose fossil remains are to be found in the oldest of lands.

Finally, even if the explorer is not a specialist, he can reveal the existence of underground works of beauty. On the earth's surface many a monument is put up and kept in repair by human hands at great expense. Underground, nature has preserved, and is still freely building, huge cathedrals and elaborate galleries, embellished in infinite variety. Many are already well known, and some are positively jewels, attracting crowds of sight-seers every year, but there are many more yet to be discovered.

This short summary of speleological activities only gives a hint of the importance that underground exploration can have in limestone regions. To round off this preface, let us take the single example of Pierre Saint-Martin.

Owing to lack of water and the progressive destruction of vegetation by sheep, the limestone plateaus dominating Sainte-Engrâce, and stretching far beyond it, have practically become deserts. At Sainte-Engrâce itself, lack of electric power makes life hard for the population and prevents the creation of local industries. Water is abundant, but it issues out too low to be of use either for irrigating the plateaus or for producing electricity. The exploration of Pierre Saint-Martin shows that the large underground river in the cave comes out at the springs of Benta (1,440 feet) in the Kakouetta gorge. This channel, running from 5,740 feet (the height of the cave) down to 1,440 feet, involves a downgrade of 4,300 feet, which probably makes it at this moment the biggest fall of its kind in the world. The underground river, discovered in the depths, has a rate of flow of over 3 cubic feet per second. If its waters were collected by a lateral tunnel they would add up to a fall of 2,300 feet. It can easily be calculated how much energy, running at least into several tens of millions of kilowatt-hours a year, could be produced from a fall of this size.

This discovery is capable of changing the hydroelectrical resources and the economic development of an entire region; it shows that in estimating the potential electrical energy of France, the contribution of underground rivers ought to be taken seriously into account. It also shows, without need of further proof, how important speleologists' expeditions can be.

FELIX TROMBE
Director of Research
National Center of Scientific Research

Foreword

IT WAS a wide, high, weather-beaten country of limestone and twisted pines, set in the farthest corner of France, where the Basque mountains emerge from their woods and meadows, rearing up so ruggedly that only a corroded boundary stone is needed to turn the nameless wilderness into Spain. In the summer months, white and brown sheep, their fleeces thick and their horns long and curling, are driven up here by the shepherds of Aramits and Arette. Protected by their goatskins from the winds, and leaning on their long crooks, the shepherds stand gazing at the vultures and eagles that circle above the valleys, under a lofty sky, swimming with feathery silvered clouds. Even in summer, frequent mists enclose these steep pastures, which are filled with traps curiously contrived by sinkholes in the rocks. It is a waste of cloud, rain and squall; a no man's land, equally foreign to both the countries it divides.

Lower down, toward the north, narrow winding gorges have been hollowed out, bearing names as wild as their nature—Holçarté and Kakouetta. Alive with sudden streams, these gorges abound in waterspouts,

19

gushing from their precipitous, rocky sides. What can be the source of this astonishing wealth of water? If one could only see through the walls from which it cascades, thundering and iridescent, follow up its meanderings and track down its subterranean courses, sharing its adventures, through the heart of the perforated rock, right up to its hidden springs, deep in the earth's mass. . . .

For many years, Max Cosyns and his friends had been striving to discover the secret of these gorges. Courage and persistence notwithstanding, they had never succeeded in penetrating very far into the chasms, for impassable flooded tunnels, or "siphons," held up their progress. They had, therefore, turned their attention a thousand yards upward to the ridges and plateaus, checkered with rock and grass, that received the downpours of the skies, and seemed completely to absorb them, without leaving over even a surface streamlet. What happened to all this water, and to the water made by the melting of the snows? It must surely make its way through a thousand crannies in the limestone cap, and after many wanderings in the dark, gather its forces to burst out at last in the gorges below.

Max Cosyns's group set themselves the task of traversing the entire rough country dominated by the misty silhouettes of the peaks of Arlas and Anie. One day, when two of the speleologists, Georges Lépineux and Giuseppe Occhialini, were taking a rest, not far from the old frontier post called Pierre Saint-Martin, Lépineux saw a crow apparently emerging in full flight from a rock. It was at the bottom of a doline, a sort of large shaft, which for some ten yards made a jagged hole in the flank of a steep valley. Lépineux was an observant man, and, like Newton after watching the apple fall, he was for a long time lost in thought. If the crow had come out of the rock, it must be because there was a hole there with a nest in it. Now, crows only build their nests in places where there is a clear drop beneath them. And such clear drops, concealed in the recesses of the mountains, were exactly what the speleologists were looking for; they quickly climbed down the ten yards of cliff, and running to the rock wall, discovered a pothole; widening it, they flung down pebbles that were lost within the dizzy reaches of an abyss. The chasm of Pierre Saint-Martin had been discovered.

That was in 1950. The first descent was undertaken in the following summer. Though I had never before penetrated into a cave, I agreed to take part, yielding to the persuasions of my friends who wanted pictures taken which would record the experiences of this first expedition. So it was, at the beginning of August, 1951, while the bright rocks and the twisted pines were broiling in the sun, that I came to plunge into the depths of the earth.

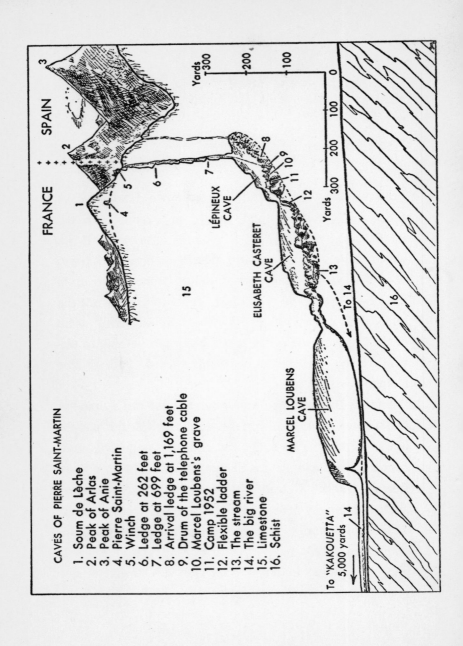

CAVES OF PIERRE SAINT-MARTIN

1. Soum de Lèche
2. Peak of Arlas
3. Peak of Anie
4. Pierre Saint-Martin
5. Winch
6. Ledge at 262 feet
7. Ledge at 699 feet
8. Arrival ledge at 1,169 feet
9. Drum of the telephone cable
10. Marcel Loubens's grave
11. Camp 1952
12. Flexible ladder
13. The stream
14. The big river
15. Limestone
16. Schist

FRANCE   SPAIN

Yards 300 — 200 — 100 — 0   100   200   300   Yards

LÉPINEUX CAVE

ELISABETH CASTERET CAVE

MARCEL LOUBENS CAVE

To 14

To "KAKOUETTA"
5,000 yards   14

I

At the bottom of the chasm, August, 1951

I DID not know how long I had been down. It would have taken a slight effort to disengage my watch from the three sleeves that covered it, and the effort seemed not worth while. It was cold; or rather, to be exact, I was cold. Drops of water were tumbling from above upon the stone; trickles of water were echoing throughout the huge, dark cavern; except for the faint slithering noise of the big reel, which for ages I had been helping to unwind, those were the only sounds I could hear in this strange world.

Silently I swore, for I had let myself get wet. Lépineux had warned me that during the second half of the descent it was impossible to dodge the countless waterfalls, and Jackie Ertaud had echoed his advice. I should have been wearing rubber overalls, but now it was too late to borrow them. By the dim light of a pocket torch, I could see at close quarters only my reel of telephone wire, the patches of rubble near by and, beyond, the vague outlines of gigantic boulders. The rest was darkness; not

25

even dark, but black, and I knew it stretched out to eternity.

I recalled my earlier experiences of the mineral world, gained among high mountains and volcanoes, inexpressively tragic in their power. Up among them, as down here, there was nothing but rock. But, up above, at least there had been light; here was nothing but stone, water and darkness. I put out my torch, and the minutes passed. I could feel them passing as the wire steadily slipped through my fingers, up toward the distant surface of the earth. Minutes went by. My eyes could pick out nothing whatever, not even the palm of my hand, held so close to my face that it almost touched my nose.

Suddenly the wire stopped running. It had been arranged that if a stoppage lasted for more than a few dozen seconds, I should get into touch with the surface.

"Hello?"

No reply. What could be happening?

I checked the connections and reversed the plugs, but to no effect. The ground seemed all right, for, as Cosyns had suggested, I had buried in damp sand the steel spike and the piece of scoured wire that acted as my ground. In order to find this damp sand, I had even had to abandon the relatively dry spot, sheltered by an overhang of the great rock face, where Ertaud had pitched his camp that evening and where all my belongings were stored.

"Hello, hello?"

Still no reply. I was not at all worried, feeling only the kind of slight irritation one experiences in towns when waiting for a delayed answer to a telephone call. This had nothing in common with the agony that had gripped me some hours earlier when, in the course of my descent, the cable had unexpectedly jammed. Those had been anxious minutes. Nobody had explained the reasons for the stoppage, and only my own calls, echoed from the precipitous rocks, had replied to me. I was hanging in space, 650 feet beneath the earth's surface and 500 feet from the bottom, my body dragged backward by the weight of the equipment attached to my shoulders, and my legs stretched out horizontally, barely at tiptoe touching the walls; time seemed interminable, while my companions above, bent over the winch, were no doubt doing everything in their power to put an end to my predicament. What if the five millimeters of twisted strands, of which my cable was formed, should break in the darkness?

At last the voice I had been waiting for spoke: "Hello, Tazieff?"

"Yes, what's happened?"

"Nothing; all's well. We've just changed shifts on the winch pedals."

"Thank heavens! But you might give me a warning before you cut off!"

A little later, crouching about 1,200 feet underground, carefully watching the unwinding of the wire as it went up, I began to think of those on top, my companions who were on the winch, or busy with wood, water and kitchen details, all concentrating on a single end—the success of the team, always personified by "the chap at the bottom." As the "chap at the bottom," I felt how intimately I was bound to them, how utterly dependent upon their courage and devotion. I thought of Janssens, pedaling on the winch the equivalent of 90 miles a day. Not only his feet, but his hands were at work, turning the second crank that was coupled by chains to the pedals. I could envisage him, earphones on head and cigarette stub in mouth, winding and pedaling for hours on end.

It was then that I began to feel really cold. My teeth chattered like castanets. I would have liked to give up watching the wire unwind, and to have moved across to the camp, which was some yards to my right. I lit an acetylene lamp, hungry for its warm, yellow, glowing flame, and I also set alight a box of solidified alcohol. This would warm me a little, and I should be able to boil some water for tea. . . . But I found that the reel was only two-thirds unwound. Perhaps three-quarters, I hoped, fingers crossed.

From time to time my jaws seemed to lock. Then there would be a moment of relief, followed by another bout of lockjaw. I felt like an exhausted boxer, for whom the time between rounds is all too brief. And to think that I could be lying up above under a burning sun in the midst of the most wonderful mountains! I had known I would not like it—this potholing!

Scarcely twenty days ago I had spent the night 40 yards from the crater of Stromboli, out of which, every quarter of an hour, poured a roaring white-hot sheet of fire. For miles around there had been no other human being, and conditions had certainly been more dangerous than my present ones. Nevertheless, I had not experienced the feeling of miserable impotence that possessed me now.

On a volcano, a mountain, or in a desert, whether of sand or ice, will power and fortitude have saved the life of many a man. In this pothole my safety did not depend on me. If, for some reason, the help of the team on the surface failed me, I should need wings, not only to reach the skylight, 230 feet above my head, in the roof of the underground cavern, but also to fly up the perpendicular tunnel. Its walls were slippery and glistening with water, and over great distances there was no foothold for climbing, and no convenient cleft into which a peg could be hammered. At the cost of a most exhausting descent, I had been lowered down into the depths of this chasm, and I should only get out again with the good will of those on top.

However . . . what an astonishing feeling it is to know that one is 1,200 feet underground! In mines, I had, indeed, descended lower, but there the conditions are quite different.

The wire stopped, and I plugged in.

"Hello, Tazieff, can you hear me?"

"Yes."

"We've hauled up the cable. Are you all right?"

"Yes."

"Well, I'll switch off. Loubens is just coming down. *Au revoir.*"

Suddenly a familiar noise made me pull my thoughts together: it was a stone ricocheting against the walls of the shaft. In two or three seconds it burst out noisily into the darkness, somewhere quite near, followed by a whistling fall of shale.

Gathering up in my arms the big reel and its stand, I rushed toward the site of my camp. Behind this great stone boulder, shaped like a railway van, I should find some protection. Slipping on the slope, I stumbled two or three paces on my knees, stood up again, and at last reached safety. Hurriedly, I set up the reel, propping it up with heavy pieces of rubble. My wire had gone slack, and I began to unravel it, hoping there would be no knots.

More stones hurtled against the sides of the shaft, and were shattered in pieces upon the huge rock bottom, not far away. Loubens must have covered the first 260 feet, and these would be pieces of rock dislodged and shot into the void by his descent of the great terrace that sloped at an angle of 40 degrees.

Fathom after fathom, I hauled the wire in and wound it up. Time was passing—but I could not tell whether slowly or quickly. Now and again there was a stoppage, lasting sometimes seconds and sometimes minutes. I thought of Loubens, waiting under icy jets of water, for the men at the top to set him in motion again. About 4 yards a minute is the average speed of descents and ascents. When the human spider, coming down his thread,

1951: Marcel Loubens is ready to go down on his first descent into the caves of Pierre Saint-Martin. On this expedition the world record up to that time for a perpendicular descent was broken—1,155 feet down, the first of the enormous underground caverns was discovered. Here Loubens is poised over the preliminary straight drop of 1,000 feet. A tremendous effort is needed to pull men up and down the vertical shaft. The electric winch was not used until the following year. (*J. Ertaud*)

Here Jean Janssens, a member of the 1951 expedition, pedals the windlass. Ventures into the interior of the earth require much equipment, the concentrated energy of many men, as well as a true feeling of team spirit, especially in critical moments of danger. In 1940, only close teamwork together with miraculous luck saved Marcel Loubens and his companion, both injured, from death in the cave of Henne-Morte. It was the latter exploration which caused Loubens to catch the "speleological bug," the desire to investigate one cave after another. (*J. Ertaud*) 551.44   3990

T

finds a narrow traverse, he asks for a halt to revive his numbed limbs and ease his ribs, crushed by the vicelike grip of his harness. But there are other interruptions as well: changes of shift on the pedals, and technical break-downs. These always occur at the most inconvenient mo-ments—when one is suspended in open space, far from the surface of the walls, ceaselessly spinning on the end of a wire that is stretched out stiff as a rail.

While somewhere up above Loubens's mysterious de-scent went on, signaled to me only by the continual roll-ing in of the wire through my fingers and, now and again, by a shooting pebble, whistling like a cannon ball, I had time to reflect upon the extraordinary exertions that speleology demands of its addicts.

We had spent a week getting ready for the descent. In front of a sort of narrow window, leading into the chasm, the team had built a flat bank of dry stones. The winch was set up and meticulously trimmed by Pérot, Cosyns, Janssens and Petitjean. Then, for two days, they had mixed mortar, and cemented the shale and scree and broken overhanging boulders that lined the exit of the chasm, and which might have proved dangerous. Labey-rie, Lévi and Occhialini had checked the equipment, folded and rolled ladders and ropes, inspected the lamps

and torches and prepared the rations for those who were
going below.

Then there had come a day of tests, and another in
which the winch was put in position. All the time the
weather had been filthy, with persistent drizzle and thick
mist—and I, in my innocence, had expected the Pyrenees
to be parched and broiled in the sun!

I had wanted to take pictures of the descent of
Lépineux, the first man to take off for the bottom of the
chasm he had himself discovered. And so I had been
posted 262 feet down on a ledge, 6½ feet wide by 26
feet long, from which, at the slightest movement, scree
and debris were hurled into the darkness. That day, the
sun shone in a cloudless sky, but we had no chance to
see it, except early in the morning and late at night. I
spent seven hours, crouched against a sticky rock wall,
hardly daring to move after Lépineux had passed me
and was exposed to the fall of stones. Soaked to the skin,
I learned by yelling up to the surface—for I had no other
means of communication—that after an hour and forty-
seven minutes, Lépineux had beaten the world record
for a perpendicular descent. He had gone down to 1,155
feet and discovered a cave big enough to hold the whole
of Notre-Dame de Paris.

After many long hours, Lépineux emerged once more;

seen, as I saw him, in the yellow glow of acetylene, he looked exhausted, his face drawn and his eyes dilated.

I can still hear his words: "It was wonderful. . . . Wonderful . . ."

Then, when he had stretched his legs on my narrow terrace, he shouted through the throat-microphone: "All right! You can haul me up."

An hour later I, too, was hauled up, and Jackie Ertaud was being lowered into the depths. After an unusually quick descent, during which he never asked for a halt, Ertaud spent the night alone below, taking photographs. When he was hoisted up at eight o'clock next morning, his features were worn and exhausted, but he had the radiance of a man greeting the dawn after a good night's work.

As on the day before, the weather was superb, and I would gladly have stayed on the surface to take full advantage of the elusive sun, but now it was my turn to plunge into the chasm. Within a few seconds I was being lowered out of the dry warmth, to which I had so much looked forward, into the engulfing dampness of the caves. Potholing is, indeed, a strange passion; I was beginning to understand what it meant—darkness, damp and waiting. . . .

Meanwhile, the wire was still coiling up, and I was

still rolling it in. At last, far away and distorted by re-verberating echoes, the voice of Loubens came to me; with the aid of the throat-microphone he was trying, from above me, to make himself understood, although without much success.

The second time I heard him, he seemed nearer, and soon I could distinguish his words, and his characteristic Gascon accent: "Everything's fine. I'm window-shopping. The walls are smooth as glass, and my nose is glued to them!"

I waited a moment, and then I shouted: "Hi! Loubens!"

"Tazieff! I'm bored stiff. How much farther is it?"

"I can't see you, but you must have reached the ceiling of the cavern. Is your torch on?"

"Of course."

With one hand I was trying to assemble my photographic equipment, the tripod, the magnesium flares and the rest. After hours and hours of unvarying darkness, here at last was a beam of light—Loubens's head lamp. He had just passed through the roof of the cavern.

"Tazieff, I can see your torch. Thank heavens, we've done it!"

And the yellowish light, like a glowworm's, set in my companion's helmet, was bobbing up, vanishing, bobbing up and vanishing again. I let go the wire, seized my gear and hurried across to be in time for his landfall. Naturally I tripped, fell on my knees and got up, only to trip once more. But at last I was there. Carefully I set up my camera and arranged the lights. The supply I had been given had run so low that I dared not use more than three flashes for these shots. I was not at all happy about it. Next time, I decided, I would look after lighting myself. I arranged the flares in a cluster, their fuses touching, and lay in wait.

Outside the halo cast by my own head lamp, I could see nothing whatever. Then, suddenly, within the range of my battery of lights, there appeared a vague and scarcely perceptible shape. The match I was holding crackled and flared. I put it to my three fuses; they took, and a dazzling light burst forth. Turning round, I grasped the camera and pressed the knob. Though I had been nearly blinded by the brilliance of the lights, Loubens, who was hardly a dozen yards away, spinning on his cable as he slowly neared the bottom, seemed only a dim silhouette against a black background. My flares, I knew, lasted for a minute and a half; that is the equivalent of a 20- or 25-foot descent.

Clothed in a dark green waterproof flying suit, he came gradually down. He was hanging from his belt, his legs wide apart, raised a little, and his hands drawn in on his stomach. I could see nothing of his face, which was looking upward, and the rest of his head was concealed by a metal helmet. He seemed an eerie and terrifying robot.

The robot touched the top of one of the huge boulders that jut out of the floor of the cavern, and at once came to life.

"Stop!"

The cable halted, but Loubens could not stand up on his precarious platform.

"Come down another 3 yards," I advised.

He spoke to the surface, and again began to advance, on the end of his cable, his back to the slope, gently buffeted by the boulders like a diver, none too skilled, stumbling on the floor of the sea.

"Well, there you are! How was it?"

"My ribs are aching. That harness is terribly tight."

"Don't worry about that. Now you're here, I can get on with things. In this place one's blood freezes up."

"I've certainly arrived just in time; it's getting dark, and I might have been held up."

I had forgotten that in some parts of the world it does, indeed, get dark and again grow light.

We went down to the camp. Loubens took off his bag,

Lépineux leaves for the bottom on the 1951 expedition. He discovered the entrance to the Pierre Saint-Martin caves by searching for the nest of a crow which he had observed flying out of apparently solid rock. Attached to his helmet is an acetylene lamp; the flexible metal ladder, with aluminum rungs, is designed for light carrying. In every cave exploration the success of the team is measured only by the progress of the man or men down below. Lépineux was now on his way to discover the secret underground streams which burst out thousands of feet lower down in the gorges of Kakouetta and Holcarté. (*J. Ertaud*)

Our camp in the Pyrenees, 1951, "a weatherbeaten country of limestone and twisted pines set in the farthest corner of France . . . a waste of cloud, rain and squall . . . a no man's land." Max Cosyns and his friends spent many years in this rugged district trying to fathom the secrets of the underground streams. Soil erosion began to wear the region down severely around the era of Louis XIV—formerly, beech and pine forests covered the upper slopes. (*J. Ertaud*)

In a shepherd's cabin, from left to right: Loubens, Tazieff and Lépineux. Tazieff was then a newcomer to speleology. He had done most of his geological work as a student, at perilously close range, of volcanoes, and as an alpinist. Nearly all speleologists are sportsmen, requiring physical skill, strength and adroitness. But their work has immense practical and scientific applications. (*J. Ertaud*) stuffed full of equipment. He hesitated before unbuckling the straps of his harness. I had done the same; for one has to remember how to refasten it properly for the ascent, making sure that the special buckle is correctly locked. It is enough to make one shudder even to think of that buckle coming apart in mid-air. We carefully examined the harness's pattern, memorizing the position of each strap.

"That's all right."

And now he was free from the vicelike grip that for the last two hours had squeezed his ribs and thighs. There was a moment of relaxation. I went to fill a mess tin from one of the near-by streamlets, and Loubens boiled the water. We went over our supplies and equipment, sorted them out and arranged them. By my watch, it was 6 P.M.; I had been underground seven and a half hours, and done nothing but wind up wires and cables.

"Underground," Loubens told me, "time doesn't matter. You'll be surprised."

In fact, whether we were at work or merely waiting, time glided by remarkably quickly. Which is very strange, for I had always imagined that in cold, darkness, and during long uncomfortable periods of inactivity, time would have seemed interminable. But what is time? Numbed by the damp cold of the caves, my mind groped vainly

toward an understanding of why six hours can pass
so much more rapidly than the terrifying second of a
fall through space, and why a year in an adult's life seems
so short compared with the endless hour of a boring
classroom when one is twelve, and the June sun is shining outside.

Loubens brought me back to reality. "Well, what do
you think of it?"

This was my baptism as an amateur of caves. What
did I really think?

"Hm . . . I can only wonder what's stung you. You
mean to say that every summer you have yourself lowered into places like this for pleasure?"

But no one should dispute about tastes.

At last the water had boiled. Careful not to burn our
mouths, we drank our sweet mixture of coffee and preserved milk, gratefully feeling its warmth spread through
our chilled limbs.

"What do you want to eat?" Loubens asked. "Forti-
fied biscuits, vitaminized paste or chocolate?"

The thought of this scientifically prepared and phar-
maceutically proportioned food was enough to take away
my appetite. I thought nostalgically of a hunk of bread,
a slice of cheese and a glass of red wine. Less hard to

please, Loubens was conscientiously munching his chocolate.

"What shall we do next?" he asked abruptly.

"Let's finish with the photographs, and then we can go exploring."

"Good!"

Loubens was heart and soul a photographer. As soon as he had had enough money, his earliest extravagance had been to buy the latest model in cameras. And so we got on very well together; he never grudged a few minutes, if they were devoted to taking pictures. In any case, we live in an age when every discovery, adventure and out-of-the-ordinary voyage ought to be recorded on film.

Loubens raised his voice and called the men on top. "Hello, Lévi! Loubens here. We're staying the night down below."

"All right. Contact at 6 A.M. tomorrow."

"Thanks! Good night."

Slowly he took off his headphones and unhooked the fastenings of the throat-microphone from behind his neck. For eleven hours we were to be isolated from the rest of the world.

II

Record depths

LOADED with equipment, we set off on our expedition. It was a stiff slope of heavy gravel, but the going was easy. Our acetylene lamps had been recharged, and could cast a light as far ahead as 50 yards. The path led between two rows of rock, formed by huge boulders wedged together in unearthly shapes. As we went, the shifting beams of our lamps evoked an outlandish ballet of light and shadow upon a background, reddish and pale gray stone.

We had made the circuit of our castle keep and, having turned back to the left, were now hugging the left wall of the cavern.

"Jackie has been working here," Loubens declared.

On the ground were broken flash bulbs, glittering dimly amid red-and-white spotted cardboard boxes. We were picking our steps carefully in this stony maze, threading our way through vaults and buttresses, clambering over creviced boulders and slipping through the narrowest of passages.

For twelve hours, Jackie Ertaud had explored this region, observing, rummaging around, and taking photographs. As he was all alone, he had not risked taking off his parachute harness, in case he could not put it on again. This harness was strapped very tight, and it grew even tighter, as moisture was absorbed by the straps. Because of this, Jackie had been obliged to bend over double, drawing his whole body in toward the safety buckle on his stomach. It was a position painful enough when one is sitting still, but Jackie had kept it up for twelve hours and performed almost acrobatic feats.

It had seemed to him funny, at first, to be voluntarily imprisoned in an iron collar, but jokes wear off when they last for hours. He was cut off from everybody, surrounded with perils in an unknown and unexplored cave; worn out by continuous exertion, and with his nerves at a stretch, he began to make one mistake after another in his photography.

"I was so utterly exhausted," he told us when he came up, "that I started taking bad pictures deliberately. About three o'clock in the morning I had a black-out."

How many men have risked their lives alone, as he did, amid the uncharted dangers of a subterranean cavern?

In the light of our torches, a hole in the rock wall came into view, offering the prospect of untracked paths.

We climbed up to it, and found a narrow trench leading deep into the heart of the rock. Combing it with the beams of our lamps, we could see no serious obstruction.

"Shall I go through?" Loubens asked.

"Just a minute, while I take some pictures."

I had to find a stone that was flat, dry enough, and shelving at the right angle, scatter my powder and light the tiny fuse. Then I focused the camera on the gap in the rock. The explosion of the flares, lighting up the rocky framework around us, for a moment revealed the real dimensions of the cavern. And with the crackling of the burning powder was mingled the hum of the camera.

Loubens had disappeared, caught up in an elbow of the trench, into which he had slipped sideways. I stopped the camera, and took advantage of the last few seconds of light to consider what I could see of the cavern. The roof was only dimly discernible; everywhere else, illuminated in the last flickers of flame, were huge masses of rock, flanked by smaller boulders shining with moisture.

"Hi, Tazieff!"

"Yes?"

"This doesn't lead any farther. But I can hear water running."

"On the other side of the rock?"

"No. There's a cleft."

"What next?"

"I'm coming back."

Loubens reappeared.

"I don't think it can have been the wind. It must have been water. Lépineux heard it and Ertaud, too; they were sure it wasn't the wind."

"Well, that's something. Let's go on."

We set off once more, squeezing between two great, closely wedged boulders. Scaling another, we came down again, keeping our backs to the wall. I stopped before an opening in the rubble, one or two feet wide. Loubens approached and leaned over, and we exchanged glances.

"That must be the shaft that Lépineux spoke of."

I picked up a stone, stepped forward, and carefully threw it down the center of the hole.

"One, two . . . (the stone knocked against something and bounced off), three, four, five . . . That's the end."

Loubens did the same.

"One, two, three, four, five, six, seven . . ."

"This seems to be the real thing."

"Yes, but very dangerous."

The heaped-up rocks, buttressed one against the other, stood around the shaft like brooding pyramids.

"Let's look a little farther."

I was possessed by the thirst for discovery, the delight

of finding a way to penetrate still farther, and still deeper. We were now skirting the wall, which fell back to the right, toward the east, heralding the bottom of the cavern. I was walking in front, as quickly as could be done across this sort of ground. With my lamp probing into the rock, I peered into recesses and corners, anxiously looking for an opening.

"So it's got you, the potholing virus?"

"It certainly has!"

Both of us were ferreting among the boulders, on all sides, like spaniels in a thicket.

"Oh, come and see!"

I climbed a boulder, and let myself slide down its other face. Loubens was bending over a kind of hole, a yard or two wide, surrounded by stones that looked firm and steady. Ten feet lower down was a terrace, and after that a precipitous drop. We threw pebbles, counting the seconds—four, five, six. . . . Loubens had pursed his lips and was softly whistling with pleasure.

In a few minutes, we had cleared out the entrance. I took the rope out of my pack, and Loubens fastened himself to it. Firmly secured, he let himself slip into the shaft where, without any trouble, he reached the terrace. Leaning over the gulf he circled it with the beam of his head lamp.

"Anything to see?"

"Thirty-five feet down there's a great slope of rubble; but everything looks decayed and rotten."

He broke off a few stones, and I could hear them bounding and rolling about in the lower regions. The echoes seemed to issue from other points in our cavern, as if its bottom were perforated with holes. More stones went clattering down and again the reverberations rose around me.

"It sounds very promising," I said. "Will you go down or shall I?"

"It's dangerous, very dangerous."

With the rope stretched round my back and my left shoulder, I peered into the shaft, my legs wide apart. Loubens was carefully probing the rocks, leaning over, turning back and reaching out again, farther to the right.

"If only you could see what we're standing on. I believe if I pushed over one of these blocks of stone, the whole heap would go tumbling down. It's frightening."

I knew he was right by the tone of his voice. I recognized man's fear when confronted by the terrible powers of nature—the fear that grips your stomach when you are in a region constantly bombarded by volcanic eruptions, or that seizes you when you cross a belt of scree, knowing that at any moment you may start an avalanche under your foot. It is the fear of being crushed and buried beneath thousands of tons of crashing rock.

I said nothing. It was for Loubens to work out the chances, and decide for himself what should be done.

"Will you pass me the ladder?"

"I'll make the rope fast, and hand it down."

I took our tightly rolled ladder out of my pack. Instead of ropes, it had thin steel strands; and, instead of wooden rungs, hollow tubes of light alloy. At each end, metal rings were attached to its cables. I passed a snap hook through them and, with the aid of a ring of steel wire, firmly anchored them to a solid jut of rock. In a moment, the ladder was hanging down into the void.

"Right, I'm off," said Loubens. "If I don't come back, look after Patrick for me."

Grasping the ladder, he cautiously went down rung after rung, and disappeared from sight. I could follow his progress, however, by the rope I was holding and paying out, and by the gentle vibrations of the ladder. Three feet and a halt; another 3 feet and another halt. It took a long time. Then my friend's voice reached me, not from up the shaft, but as if rising from under my feet.

"This is extraordinary! If only you knew what is under your feet. The whole thing holds up by a miracle." After a short silence, he added, "And I don't believe in miracles!"

The ladder was quivering again. I could hear Loubens breathing, and a few seconds later he was standing beside me. Fatigue was beginning to make itself felt, but we now knew that beneath us was a chasm into which, at all costs, we had to find a way.

It must have been midnight when at last we discovered an opening, tucked away between the main wall of the cavern and two huge adjoining boulders. Prudence prevailed, however, and we decided to go back to the camp to rest and drink some coffee. The hot coffee tasted very much better than it had at 6 P.M. Loubens nibbled at some of what he called his scientific food. Then we were ready for action.

It was easy to begin with. We slipped between two boulders, and threaded our way under a third. A few paces more between the rubble and the roof, and there we were. The shaft was much like any other, but less accessible. We cleared out the entrance and shook out the ladder into the abyss. Loubens went down the rungs 35 feet, smoothly and without hesitation.

"It's a few more yards yet. Will you pay out the rope?"

Inch by inch, I let the rope slip slowly through my hands. Loubens touched bottom.

"I'm on a steep slope, a slope of rubble. Please make fast!"

Coming to the end of the rope, Loubens unhitched himself.

"Fine!" he shouted, "the usual gradient, 30 to 40 degrees, just like the first cave. This is even bigger, I'd say. I'm going on down."

"Shall I come down after you?"

"No. You wait."

And apprehensively I waited.

"It's astonishing. The rock bed is quite fantastic."

In his enthusiasm, he drew out the syllables of the word "fantastic," and they went echoing from rock to rock. A few seconds passed.

"It's huge, positively huge. I've switched on the large torch, but, even so, I can't see the walls. I'm going down a little farther."

Step by step, he plunged on. Every thirty seconds we hailed one another, "Oo-hoo." Soon he was too far off to speak to me, and his "oo-hoos," getting fainter and fainter, were the last link between us.

I stood still, impatiently waiting for him to come back, so that I, too, could take a share in exploring this gigantic cavern. But he plunged on, deeper and deeper.

After awhile I could hear him no longer, and there was no answer to my cries.

"It's all right," I thought. "He must be going round the back of one of those great boulders. . . . I'll be hearing him again in a moment."

But the minutes got longer, and the silence grew more and more heavy.

"Not round the back of a boulder. Perhaps he's walked into a side gallery. . . ."

Regularly I let out a loud "oo-hoo," listened, counted up to thirty and shouted again. When Loubens left me I had looked at my watch. It was then 3:13 A.M.; now it was 4:05 . . . 4:10, 4:15, 4:30. Would I have to take care of Patrick? 4:40. By nature, I am an optimist, but now my optimism was wilting. I could feel it dying away like the flame of the lamp I had placed on a rock. A thousand accidents that might have happened sprang to my mind. Five o'clock. What should I do? If he had lost himself, I should surely hear his cries.

I was longing to go down myself, not now for the sake of exploring. But in that huge cave, I should hardly stand a chance of finding Loubens. And even if I found him, what could I do? Nothing, if he were dead; and if he were injured, not very much, for it would be impossible to carry him up again alone.

There was nothing for it but to wait, and, while waiting, to shout at intervals, in case he had simply got lost. If he had not reappeared by 5:30, I could go back to camp; it had been arranged that we should call the surface at exactly 6 A.M. Then I should have to ask for help. Labeyrie could come down, Janssens and the rest —they were all reliable fellows.

I do not know whether I shook with emotion when far off I suddenly heard Loubens shouting, after an hour and a half of silence. But my reply was a howl of joy. And Loubens's voice came nearer.

"Tazieff, where are you?"

"Here!"

"Yes, but where?"

"In the Place Vendôme, you ass! Where do you think? At the entrance to the cave!"

"But I can hear you from four different sides. This place is full of echoes."

What could I do in the circumstances but try one point of the compass after another, in the hope of hitting on the right one? I told him what I was doing, shouted more frequently, and lit one of our last magnesium flares.

Loubens groped in one direction, then in another. Suddenly I heard him: "Tazieff! I can see your light. That's it, I recognize the slope. I'm utterly exhausted."

The Pyrenees have been in existence for millions of years. During all this time rain water and melting snows have been dripping and eating channels through the surface of the rock. Here the front of a limestone massif clearly shows the ravaging effects of weathering and of water erosion.

In this picture the grooves and fissures carved out by thousands of centuries of erosion are in sharp relief. In such places, watching for clues to subsurface chasms and rivers today holds more possibilities for discovery than the Antarctic, the Andes or the Himalayas. Caves are a relatively new area of exploration, with unlimited opportunities for future investigation.

A party is making its way through the gorges of Kakou-etta, one of the places where the waters of the underground river of Pierre Saint-Martin have their re-surgence. These streams, properly traced and developed, can be sources of drinking water, irrigation and electric power. The channel of this river runs down a grade of 4,300 feet, making it the biggest fall of its kind known in the world. (*J. Ertaud*)

"What have you been up to? Why couldn't I hear you?"

"Lost myself, taking notes and trying to work out the route. This is a cave, if ever there was one—1,600 feet by 1,000, can you imagine it?"

"And how high?"

"Three hundred and fifty feet."

"And at the bottom?"

"At the bottom there's a river. . . ."

The next task was to haul him in by the rope to the foot of the ladder that was dangling in the void. I heaved and pulled with all my strength, puffing and blowing like an exhausted oarsman. Then the ladder began to rock. Without exchanging a word, we concentrated on this last effort. Eventually, down below, I saw the glow of his head lamp emerging.

"Don't move. Keep still. I must get the camera."

"Hurry up," he panted. "I'm done in."

I grabbed the camera. There was no time for the tripod which was lying on the ground, folded up. But it would come in useful as a lamp stand. I stuck three magnesium flares on its legs, laid the fuses and reached for matches. The light burst out with the violence of a blow in the face. With my eye glued to the view finder, I shot a ghost of a face, drawn and emptied of all energy.

He drew himself up, stiff-jointedly, like an automaton.

Head, shoulders, torso—then he fell forward, flat on his stomach, his legs still dangling down the shaft. Seizing him round the waist, I helped him out.

"Twenty to six. We must hurry. Contact's at 6 A.M.!"
We folded up the rope and rolled in the ladder.

"We've broken the record of Henne-Morte," Loubens gasped—"1,657 feet . . . and a river, as well. . . ."

After the frightful nervous tension, brought on by endless plodding alone through total darkness—a struggle in which he had had to call upon all his will power in order to avoid giving way to despair, and at the same time continue working out his course and his position—after this great expenditure of physical and moral energy, while rolling up his ladder, Loubens broke down and wept.

III

Back to daylight, back to the dark

ONCE we had returned to the top, we hoped that the rest of the team would be able to take their spell, and push on with the task of exploration. Two or three fresh men, with good ladders, were all that was needed to reach our underground river and follow its course. But it could not be done. Our pedal winch was not strong enough. Loubens's ascent and my own had been far from comfortable: the wear and tear on the winch, of which some parts were giving way, were only equaled by the wear and tear on us.

It was broad daylight when I emerged from the depths of the doline. I had been underground for twenty-four hours, and two long hours I had spent being hauled up to the surface. Only when I reached the sloping terrace, less than 260 feet below ground, could I catch glimpses of sunlight. In a normal cave 260 feet below ground is a respectable depth. But at this point in the chasm of Pierre Saint-Martin, I felt that I was already on the outskirts of daylight. This was a country I knew, and the great adventure was over.

Twenty minutes later I made my exit. The team was waiting for me, several of them crouching over the narrow opening of the window in the rock. They gave me a cheer, and it was reassuring to feel the strength of our fellowship. I was hardly in the open before they were rushing round me, unbuckling my harness, undoing the hooks of my overalls and taking off my wet clothes. In a few moments I was almost naked under the warm sun.

"How was it? Is there really a river?"

"Of course there is. Loubens found it. I stayed in the first cavern."

I had to tell my story, explaining every detail. And to some extent, the hope of more discoveries in the future softened the blow of not being able to go down again at once.

The cable was now being unwound again to fetch up Loubens.

"I'm hungry," I told Lévi. "There's nothing but sweets and concentrates in your confounded rations."

"Never mind. Come and try a leg of lamb."

I climbed up to the dry-stone shacks of our friends, the shepherds. The sky, the light, the white clouds driven by the wind, were good to see.

"What a waste of light!"

I sat on the short grass, cropped by the sheep. Weariness was suddenly heavy upon me. In her motherly way,

Jacqueline Cosyns brought me my food; it was good, simple, solid fare—bread, fresh meat, cheese and red wine in an old seasoned wineskin.

"I don't know which is nicer, Jacqueline, eating or sleeping."

What happiness there was simply in having the sun in my eyes and on my skin!

"As for potholing—I'm glad to know what it's like, but that's enough for me!"

I scarcely understood a word that Jacqueline was saying, for I had not slept a wink for thirty-two hours. Contentedly, I munched my hunk of bread.

"I must go back to the doline. We ought to have pictures of Marcel coming up."

Three hours later I woke, stretched on my back on the short grass that was already turning yellow in the late summer. Near the shack, a few steps away, Loubens was telling his story, surrounded by the rest of the team.

"Tazieff! Have you had a good sleep? What shall we do, stay the night up here or go down to the village?"

We had spent the last ten days in these rocky highlands, 5,900 feet up. They had been ten days of mist, rain and fog, and I was longing for a big hot bath.

"Let's go down."

We strode off, together. It was seven o'clock, and the

sun was low, floating on the great sea of clouds that covered everything below 5,000 feet. Only the undulating
peaks of the mountains could be seen, peaceful and pleasant in the clear evening air.

In the best of spirits, we were walking fast. On our
right, we were leaving the *bracas*—the strange wilderness
of corroded limestone where the effect of smooth, bright
stones, deep fissures, dark cliffs and caverns, jumbled
together, was curiously monotonous. The rock in these
parts had been emaciated by erosion, and one seemed to
be gazing at the bony, fleshless skeleton of the world. It
was better not to take risks in this maze, if one was in a
hurry and the weather was misty.

Where we were hurrying downhill, a thin coating of
grassy earth covered the limestone. But for this veneer
of pasture land, the rocky wilderness would have made
still wider conquests. It was about the time of Louis XIV,
I think, that soil erosion began to devastate these regions.
Till then, thick forests of beech and pine had covered
the higher mountain slopes. But wood was needed for
building the frigates and caravels of the royal navy.
Trees were felled mercilessly, right down to the ground,
and the light soil and humus, no longer anchored by
strong roots, were swept down into the valleys by the
copious streams of this rainy country. Only grass lived

Members of the 1952 Pierre Saint-Martin expedition; from left to right, standing: Jacques Théodor, Jean Thamtham (a shepherd), Marcel Loubens, Henri Bigué-Bernasqué (another shepherd), Éric Samuel; sitting: a porter, Beppo Occhialini, Geoffrey Fertel. As often happens in speleology, this team comprised a number of different nationalities and professions.

Marcel Loubens checks over his gear before making his last fatal descent. Each man carries between 110 and 130 pounds of equipment, all essential to the maintenance of life and scientific work down below. With the electric winch, a man theoretically can be dropped down a perpendicular shaft of 350 yards in half an hour, burdened with a full load of equipment. (*Le Parisien Libéré*)

Marcel Loubens checking over his helmet and harness. The helmet is of the type used by jet pilots; the harness, made of nylon, is the latest design used by parachute troops. Always uncomfortable at best, the harness must be buckled with the utmost care to avoid injury. It is very risky for a man alone and underground to attempt to remove his harness. The actual average speed of descent or ascent when attached to the electric winch cable is four yards per minute. (*Le Parisien Libéré*) on, and here and there a pine tree, clinging to a pocket in the rock. Quite recently, a woodcutter had discovered in the forest, lower down, an interesting relic of what used to be called the mast road, the road through the valley along which chained galley slaves used to haul tree trunks to the shipyards. The relic was a *cœur-de-bronze*, a heart-shaped padlock employed to fasten the convicts' chains.

In the millions of years that the Pyrenees have existed, rain water and the melting snows have steadily dripped through the surface of the rock. A considerable body of this water has accumulated in underground lakes, issuing in the form of springs at various points on the hillsides. At other points in the rock bed, it has wound its way into deep clefts. Limestone is about the only rock that can be dissolved by water, especially if acid is present; and, trickling through the light soil, the Pyrenean waters have absorbed much acid from the humus. Thus, in the course of hundreds of thousands of years, the waters have slowly widened the limestone faults, dissolving the rock and gradually absorbing it. Grooves have been deepened and galleries hollowed out, horizontally and sloping at angles, along the geological joins. Where the waters met a particularly soluble rock bed, huge halls and caverns have been formed. There, between the surface and the bottom of the limestone stratum, which rests on impermeable schist, 4,000 feet down, the mountains have been drilled and threaded with *chantoirs*, dolines, shafts, chasms, galleries and caves of every description. So long as a thick layer of soil covered the rock, the abysses that underlay it were revealed only by occasional subsidences. But once deforestation was complete, openings appeared one after another, and the mountain waters gushed into the gaping holes. Surface streams grew fewer, and the mass of rainwater and melting snow was swallowed up within. Caves and shafts grew ever bigger, dug out by the torrents that rushed through them. Meanwhile, outside, springs and rivers dried up.

"What really attracts you speleologists, then," I was saying to Loubens, "is the chance of discovering underground rivers."

"Yes, among other things. But there are also the caves, and their beauty. Sometimes the stalactites, stalagmites and rock pools are quite magnificent. But here the interesting thing is the river; up in the mountains there are no rivers, whereas several flow out down below—through the Kakouetta gorge and the Holçarté canyon. What one wants to know is where they come from and how they get there."

"You must be pleased with what you've found."

"Pleased! I'd say so!"

For my part, I still felt that speleology had little to be said for it. I remembered, of course, the happy excitement that had possessed us when we knew the moment was at hand in which we should discover the shaft leading to the lower cavern. But I could not forget leaving behind the sun, the sky and the clouds.

A couple of miles to our left, a fine cliff reared up, sharply outlined against a clear green sky. In front of us, and very close now, was a sea of mist. We quickened our step, anxious to reach the village before nightfall. But we were to be disappointed, losing our way first on the misty hillside, and then in the woods. Surrounded by huge tree trunks, deep valleys and pale walls of rock, we had no idea where we were. Though we had just spent twenty-four hours in the caves, loaded with all sorts of lamps and flares, we had left the camp in such a hurry that we had brought no lights with us except a box of matches.

I was stupefied with fatigue, and a very long way at that moment from wanting to speculate about the place where the underground river might issue. Sleep . . . sleep! We were wet to the skin, and we could feel the cold water running down our backs, gathering in the hollows

of our belts, and then, in sudden jerks, trickling down
our hips and thighs.

"I've had enough, Marcel. I want to lie down and go
to sleep. Tomorrow morning we'll be able to see better."

"No, no. We'll soon be there."

I never knew whether he really believed we should
soon be there, or whether he was just cheering me up.
Half a dozen times he repeated the phrase, and all at
once we had really arrived. It was midnight when we
entered Sainte-Engrâce. For a fortnight our car had been
stowed away in the only available garage, belonging to
the *curé*.

"Shall we wake him up?"

"Of course we will."

The good man was not asleep, and he entertained us
with typical Basque hospitality—to such an extent that
when I took the wheel and started up along the winding
lane, I thought it wise to stay in second.

Loubens laughed, and agreed with me.

"Stay in second. Be sure you stay in second!"

We reached Licq safely about one o'clock in the morning. Walking into the hotel bar, where the dark paneling
softly gleamed, Loubens announced in his slow, racy Gascon accent:

"Madame Bouchet, now that I hold the world's record

for depth, I want a stoup of mulled wine really worthy of the occasion."

And though it was terribly late, Marguerite Bouchet prepared some mulled wine for us, strong enough to blow up a palace.

"I shall come back for the mulled wine," I muttered before falling asleep, "but you can keep your caves."

The autumn and winter went by without my giving a second thought to Pierre Saint-Martin; I have never had much time for memories, and the caves played no part in my present plans. Even when I found myself roasting in the sun on an island in the Red Sea, or helping to paint the white hull of the *Calypso* in the ovenlike harbor of Jedda, I felt no nostalgia for the cool recesses of the Pyrenees.

Then we returned to Europe, and I once more met some of my speleological friends—Janssens, Lévi, Cosyns and Loubens. They were discussing the attempt to be made that August, drawing up plans and assembling equipment. It was now a question of lowering down six or eight men, a team big enough to explore the huge caverns in detail and chart the course of the river. To be fully effective, the team must reach the bottom in the best possible shape, and so the descents had to be made both quick and comfortable. This involved a much better winch and suspension system than we had used on the first attempt. Max Cosyns took charge of preparing the winch. Thanks to Janssens, some of the mechanical parts were to be supplied by a large factory. Robert Lévi, a thin, tireless man, friendly in manner but tough, who was the recognized manager of the expedition, had already established close relations with the Air Ministry over the suspension problem: we were to be lent the latest type of parachute harness.

Little by little, as problems of equipment and projects of exploration were discussed, a growing interest in this dark pothole began to revive in me. I was cross-questioned about the cave, and my recollections were probed, all the more closely since Loubens was busy at this period with the small paper and plastics business he had just launched, and was seldom to be seen; while Jackie Ertaud, the second man to go down, was working night and day on the pictures we had brought back from our Red Sea trip with J. Y. Cousteau, and Georges Lépineux some months ago had joined Frank Liotard's antarctic expedition to Adélie Land.

So it was that I became involved. Among the reasons and pretexts I advanced to myself were the inadequacy of my picture record of the first expedition and the ex-

Loubens is on his way down the steep wall of the doline. At the bottom (see next picture), he will leave the ladder and henceforth be supported by only a five-millimeter strand of twisted cable. Men like Loubens take risks not only from a sense of adventure and in the hope of exploiting hidden water power; their discoveries often have immense value for geologists; for biologists interested in fossil remains; and for archaeologists and art experts in instances where wall paintings or the remains of primitive civilizations are found. (*Le Parisien Libéré*)

The entrance to the caves. It was here that the men took on final equipment before entering the chasm. The rocks scattered about the mouth are signs of a danger that threatens speleologists as well as alpinists: avalanche. In the steep corridors of caves, loose rock underfoot may be disturbed and bring on a shower of stone that could crush the disturber. The first perpendicular drop beyond the opening is a formidable one, going 1,000 feet down. At these depths any falling stone can become a lethal projectile. (*Le Parisien Libéré*) ceptional interest of the caves which deserved to be better known. But in fact the passion for discovery had seized me and I understood how speleology keeps its hold on its addicts; it works on them through the most active of yeasts—the lure of the unknown. Given the different circumstances the motive is the same that drove the crews of Eric the Red and Magellan out onto the vastness of the ocean, led Stanley and Fawcett through trackless, hostile jungles and still inspires polar explorers and mountaineers. Compared with the earth's surface, underground chasms have two advantages for explorers: this field of endeavor has been opened so recently that it contains far more possibilities of discovery than the Antarctic, the Andes or the Himalayas; moreover, a journey of a couple of dozen miles, or, at most, a couple of hundred, is all that is required to be already on site in a limestone region. Vercors, Causses, the Jura, the Pyrenees, the Italian Carso and the Yugoslav Karst are practically on one's doorstep. The speleologist can experience all the difficulties of an expedition into virgin country, its anguish and its triumphs, within the space of a mere week end. It is, in fact, Sunday afternoon exploring.

The attractions of the unknown and of unforeseeable difficulties are not, of course, the reasons generally current. They are always glossed over with more acceptable motives: economic purposes and scientific aims. I am willing to believe that the bait of fabulous riches enticed the sailors of Carthage and Cadiz into the open sea, drew Marco Polo across the steppes and deserts of Central Asia and lured the pioneers into the mountains of Peru and the forests of the Congo. But that was only the ostensible motive; what burned in the hearts of these men was surely the ecstasy of charting the unknown.

Speleology has not been behindhand in putting forward utilitarian, and even strategic, objectives. A simple love of revealing the unknown, and of running great risks and overcoming difficulties may not be frankly admitted. As with mountaineering in its early stages speleology has had to give itself scientific airs. And it is indeed fascinating to find at the bottom of chasms and in underground grottoes, new evidence on the formation of the earth's crust; to come across traces of primitive life and extinct animals, to try to pierce the secret of cosmic rays or to extend human knowledge of the biology of cave-dwelling life. But no one, I think, takes up speleology for these reasons alone. By contrast, many a speleologist has turned from sport to science, a real curiosity about this strange world gradually possessing him, though it was simply love of action that introduced him to it.

I do not know how other speleological teams are re-

cruited, but the Pierre Saint-Martin team was made up
from many professions and various nationalities. It was
a little like Jack's knife in the story—though the blade
and the handle had both been changed, it was still the
same knife. Since Cosyns had first explored the limestone
mountain mass on the frontiers of Béarn and the Basque
country, many different members had succeeded one another on his team. There had been English, Italians, Bel-
gians and Frenchmen, yet the spirit of the team had been
passed on to each in turn. In the present group, some
members came from the Jura, others from Gascony; a
few came from Belgium and Italy, and, of course, from
Paris: at the beginning of August they had all assembled
at Licq-Atherey in Basses-Pyrénées. To have come from
these scattered origins was no help in the preparation
and briefing of the expedition.

As spring wore on, and then summer, the project had
taken shape. The winch had been designed and worked
out by Max Cosyns. It was to be driven not by human
foot and hand, like last year's, but by an electric motor
run from a generating set. It was built in Brussels, under
its inventor's supervision. In theory, it could drop its man
down a perpendicular shaft 350 yards in half an hour.
At this speed, as many as four, and even six, descents a
day could be envisaged; thus, it was hoped that fresh

teams in sufficient numbers could be maintained at the bottom, and supplemented in easy relays.

Everyone going down would carry between 110 and 130 pounds of equipment: ladders, ropes and equipment for camping, canoeing and diving. Then a base camp was to be established at the bottom of the Elisabeth Casteret cavern, 1,640 feet deep, on the shingle beach which Loubens had reported as stretching along the edge of the river discovered by him. Whenever I visited Paris in these days, I found Robert Lévi busily negotiating with merchants and manufacturers for loans and gifts of equipment and provisions. In the two years I had known him, he had never been so active and elated as during the weeks before the team assembled. Thanks to him, we were supplied with the latest parachutist equipment, first-rate helmets, watertight overalls, rubber canoes, portable butane gas stoves, new tents and quantities of provisions, from fruit juice to fancy biscuits. Thus, we were saved large sums of money which we could ill afford, and we might also count on many comforts, during our descent and while we were at the bottom, which could not help but add to our chances of success.

As equipment, and promises of its early delivery, flowed in, our hopes of success went up by leaps and bounds. As soon as three men had reached the bottom of

the great perpendicular shaft, the first step would be to
descend and improve the passage leading to the lower
cavern, and then to carry down to the river enough equipment to set up a camp on its bank. In the meantime, other
members of the team would have joined the advance
guard, and exploration would start all over the huge
caverns, as well as along the river. So far as possible,
we would follow one or other of its rocky banks, then
our rubber canoes would come into use; with flexible
ladders we would climb over the waterfalls, and with
"Cousteau" diving suits cross the flooded tunnels, called
siphons, where the water is as high as the roof. If all
went well, we should emerge from the mountain somewhere in the Kakouetta gorge, 4,000 feet down and 3½
miles away.

Geologically, the project seemed feasible, for it was
clear that the thick limestone pancake rested, along an
inclined plane, upon a basis of impermeable schist. On
this lower level, the innumerable trickles of water, which
filtered through the limestone, must join to form the
rivers that issued into daylight at the bottom of the
gorges, where the schist showed through the limestone
layer.

"You must be an optimist," Labeyrie said, when I told
him of my calculations.

In spite of Lévi's efforts, there were still considerable expenses to be met, and we resorted to the classic expedient—selling in advance to one of the big dailies the story of our impressions and adventures. We fixed the deal by telephone, and Lévi's price was at once accepted. At the Air Ministry, we spent hours discussing the quality of parachute harnesses, and the reliability of their safety belts, with courteous technicians. In the end we chose a model that seemed good in every respect, and Lévi and I, one of us lightly built and the other heavy, were hung up in it from a traveling crane. We agreed that this chair of nylon straps was unquestionably more comfortable than last year's painful harness, which we had often cursed in the endless hours when we had hung suspended in the great shaft, while our legs first went numb, and then seemed to turn to stone.

In early August I crossed through France on my way to the Pyrenees, and for the first time a slight feeling of apprehension stirred in me at the thought of what lay before us. Of course, it is easy afterward to talk about the intuitions one has had before. However, it is true. Several times I caught myself reviewing the members of the team, and wondering which of the eleven would be least missed if it happened that he had forever to be left at the bottom. . . .

"You're an ass," I thought. "Overwork has made you gloomy."

Once again I was passing through the Saison Valley, boxed in between high ridges that were almost too green. Scattered about were the white Basque cottages, looking like Nuremberg toys set down in the midst of the meadows. There, at last, was the little winding lane and, ensconced in a recess in the valley, Licq itself, and the Hôtel des Touristes. This hotel had become a traditional rendezvous of speleologists, who for more than thirty years had been meeting here before scattering into the depths of the mountains. I thought of the classic hotel at Seiler du Zermatt before 1900, when sympathetic proprietors, who were more like friends than hotel managers, shared the hopes, triumphs and disappointments of their adventurous guests. Here, just the same, it was a real pleasure to greet again the open, friendly faces of the Bouchet family. For two days, while waiting for the rest of the team to arrive, we formed a boisterous party in the middle of the dining room.

Lévi had been here for a week, carefully taking stock of equipment in a barn. Everything had to be taken up on muleback to the col of Pierre Saint-Martin, and loading was now being organized. Tents, ladders, preserves, ropes, clothes, fruit juice, rubber boats, biscuits, magnesium flares, films, pegs, spikes, dried vegetables, tools, telephones, coffee, tea, snap hooks, sugar, salt, stoves, saucepans, noodles and chocolate were carefully packed in long cylinders made of thin plywood, covered with a plywood lid, and numbered for dispatch by Pierre Accoci, a journalist who had become almost an honorary member of our team.

In the previous year, a swarm of correspondents from the most varied newspapers had suddenly descended on us, up in the camp we shared with the shepherds. At first, we had no idea why they had come; then we had realized they had been attracted by the rumor that we might beat the world's record for depth. This idea of a depth record has, of course, only a relative significance; if natural conditions are favorable, one can sometimes go down more than 3,500 or 5,000 feet without any particular difficulty; it all depends on the lie of the shaft. On the other hand, there are a number of chimneys, no more than 1,000 or 1,300 feet deep, that are extremely hard to scale. But it was August, and the silly season. . . . I wish my friends in the newspaper profession would understand that speleology is more serious than that.

In 1952, just before we set off for the col, two reporters appeared in Licq; the politics of one were extremely left-wing, and the other belonged to the extreme right. They got on well together, and I believe they even passed one another tips—which is saying a lot in the newspaper world. There was little to tell them, except that we were packing and drawing up lists, and that Labeyrie, who was always cautious, was testing the ropes. One end he fastened to Sauveur Fouchet's jeep, and to the other, passed over a high beam, he tied a 50-gallon barrel full of sand. Very few of the old ropes, which Lévi had preserved, survived the test.

The winch had not yet arrived. It was coming from Brussels by road in two cars, driven by Max Cosyns and Jimmy Théodor. While waiting for it, we had a day of idleness. Only Lévi went on working, discussing transport problems with the muleteers of Sainte-Engrâce and Arette.

It was good to have a real day of rest. I had not taken one for months. We spent hours with Labeyrie in a meadow, throwing the discus. The astonished Basque cows soon got used to us, and went on browsing at the bottom of the field between a dry-stone wall and a green hedge. After the discus, we tried the javelin. Guillaume Bouchet let us have one—ten years ago he had very nearly won the French javelin record. And a javelin record, I suspect, is a harder thing to attain than a depth record.

While we were taking our exercises, under the mock-
ing eyes of the village youngsters, a convertible cabriolet
drew up, its driver waving his arms and gaily shouting
greetings. We should have recognized Loubens anywhere,
if only by his accent. He joined us at once, took off his
shirt, asked a few technical questions, and with all his
strength hurled the discus straight into a pat of cow
dung.

More and more members of our party were turning
up: Dr. André Mairey, with his curly hair and twisted
smile; Jimmy Théodor, bringing the winch from Brussels; he had not been with us in '51, though he was an
old member of the team. Next, there was Max Cosyns,
with the generating set and the motor. As Norbert Casteret, Jean Janssens, André Treuthard and Pierre Louis
had arrived the evening before, the team was nearly complete. Only Occhialini was missing, and since he was
coming from Brazil, a delay of twenty-four or forty-eight
hours was forgivable.

Transporting the winch from the cottages above Arette
to the col of Pierre Saint-Martin was almost a *tour de
force*. For our ultra-light winch weighed no less than 660
pounds. It was just over 6 feet long, and 3 feet in height
and breadth. The only way of taking it up to the col was
on the back of man or beast, for in many places the path

was merely a natural staircase in the rock. Mules were not strong enough for the job, and so what we wanted was a mountain horse. Lévi, fortunately, had found one of these rare creatures at Arette, in the Vert Valley, which runs parallel to Saison.

Bouchet's jeep took our equipment as far as the river-head. It was wonderful weather—tiny white clouds floated in a clear sky, against which the mountains stood out, green with woods and pastures. Outlined in the meadows, which were even greener, were a few log and plank cabins, brown and blackened with age, while pale yellow cows grazed around, their bells jingling.

At the riverhead, mules and the horse were waiting. Loading the mules was not particularly difficult, but a great deal of time and patience was needed to balance the fragile and clumsy winch on the horse's back. In the end it was fastened on, but very shakily, and a man was required on either side to keep it in place during the five hours of our ascent. This might have been a minor trial, if the path had been easy. Unfortunately, it was often only a scarcely discernible track amid a chaos of pale rock, and the overseers of the winch had to perform acrobatic feats in order to keep on a level with the horse, especially when, crossing steep gradients, the horse suddenly quickened its pace. Pierre Louis, Treuthard and

Lévi took turns on its port side. On the starboard, a
blond Béarnais with blue eyes, who was its owner, performed gymnastic prodigies.

Once we had passed through the woods, we were in a
region of high extensive pastures, dotted with dolines
and subsidences of earth. Our caravan stretched out
along the tops of the ridges. We skirted the extraordinary
limestone wilderness of Grand Bracas and, in sight of
the col, after circling round the base of the Arlos peak,
we met our old friends the shepherds—first, the Thamtham brothers, then Henri, and next Vincent Lagrace,
nicknamed the Judge, who was to be our patient and
kindly host in this harsh country. A big mustached man,
thin but indefatigable, and with piercing eyes beneath
his eternal black beret, he was a most generous host, al-
lowing us the entire use of two out of his three dry-stone
shacks. Even in the third, where he himself lived, he
took some of us in to lodge.

The days that followed were filled with orderly activity.
As soon as the tents were up, everyone had his own task;
it was a matter of transporting our gear to the site, and
installing the machines. The shepherds' huts were built
immediately below the level of the limestone ridge, where
they would be sheltered from the north wind. A very
steep slope of rocks and short grass stretched down to

a little valley, 200 yards below. Halfway up the side was a pit, some 10 yards wide, and in its wall the entrance to the caves gaped like a window.

Gradually the winch, the motor, the generating set, the ladders and cement, were set in place on the edge of the doline. The winch was a beautiful sight—a thoroughbred job of dull steel, with gleaming polished blocks. This precision tool was the object of all our care and attention. When we had had to carry it by hand down from the col, everyone had turned out; a dozen pairs of hands, some strong and some not so strong, had grasped the beechwood stand on which it was set, and the whole team abreast had slowly borne it down the slope. Cosyns refused to let anyone else but himself lay the stones that were to form its base, or cement them. This was a laborious task which took him more than a day. Then, when the cement was dry, this hundredweight of steel was lifted by six or seven men, and gently deposited on its pedestal.

Fifty yards higher up, in the hollow of another doline, Pierre Louis, Jimmy, Mairey and Treuthard assembled the various parts of the generating set and put it in running order. A cable was laid down to the winch, a dead, twisted pine serving as a pylon. The electric motor was to work the winch by means of a shaft more than 3 feet long, and it took no little time to adjust all this machinery. From the limestone ledges that broke up the green of the grass with a grayish white, we watched the engineers at work.

"An electric winch," Loubens said, "that ought to make for a comfortable drop."

"In theory, you'll reach the bottom in half an hour," Jimmy remarked.

"Only half an hour," I put in, "and with a harness that's the last word in luxury."

"With this gear," Marcel said, "getting down the shaft is just a formality. Unless we meet difficulties at the bottom, it'll be no more trouble than a trip in a lift."

In one of the huts our general manager had finished presiding over the classification of ropes, ladders, lamps, diving suits and rubber canoes. The orderly mass of equipment was truly impressive; it looked like an arsenal before a battle. The second shack was piled up with boxes of noodles and sardines, baskets of onions and peppers, cases of eggs, packets of biscuits and gingerbread. From beams, blackened by many decades of smoke, were hung sides of bacon and ham. And the ancient hearth, made of a few flat stones, was furnished with a clean modern stove in shining blue.

The days went by. Except for the fatigue parties and the engineers, there was no more work. Pierre Louis, who was a thin, gnarled man, with a lively, gentle face

Back in camp, Norbert Casteret, the grand old man of French speleologists, is concocting a dinner dish. He is a man of dry humor and a prolific writer. Many of his hazardous adventures below the ground were shared with his wife, Elisabeth, after whom one of the huge caverns of Pierre Saint-Martin is named. (*Labeyrie*)

The author dressed for his descent. He wears woolen underclothes, woolen shirt and sweater, trousers, linen overalls, a waterproof overall, helmet and harness. Still to be added are lamps and batteries, earphones, throat-microphone and two heavy bags of equipment. The waterproof overall is an important protection against the underground waterfalls through which the descent of the second half of the chasm is made. (*Labeyrie*)

Loubens is reaching the bottom. His previous record for perpendicular descent was established at the cave of Henne-Morte. This time he bettered his own record by discovering, 1,657 feet down, an underground hall of huge dimensions: 1,600 feet by 1,000 feet, and 350 feet from ceiling to floor, along which a river flowed. After this extraordinary find, Loubens broke down and wept. He was fated never to see the larger cavern which he correctly predicted lay farther down below. (*H. Tazieff*) under the upturned peak of his khaki cap, toiled away with sure hands under the guidance of Max Cosyns. Cosyns himself literally brooded over his machine, his long body, and long features, perpetually draped over it. Always spare with his words, he had a particularly absent-minded look whenever the winch was out of his sight.

André Mairey had arranged his drugs, medicines, bandages, splints and instruments. Like us, he was agog to get down to the caves. We were all impatience for the preparations to be over so that the real expedition could begin.

In little groups we talked over plans. What should be the order of descent? Should those have priority who had not been able to get down to the caves last year because of the failure of the winch? Everyone should have a turn, that was only fair. But it was clear that the first to go down this year must be a man in perfect condition, and with great experience in speleology.

At last we could begin to make tests. Loubens, according to rotation, was not due to go down to the bottom till last, but he volunteered for the preliminary trial. He got ready, wearing an impressive jet pilot's helmet, a khaki nylon parachute harness, a head lamp, and another lamp on his chest, a pack on his back, and hammer, spikes, and snap hooks fastened to his belt. While I helped Marcel into this complicated outfit, three or four newspaper photographers took pictures. One of them came forward almost on his knees, holding his camera as if he were going to machine-gun us. Courteously, Marcel assumed a smile. Then the smile vanished, giving way at once to the set gravity that overcomes the bravest and most experienced of men when the time has once more come to plunge into the darkness. Between the winch and the counterblock at the opening of the chasm, the thin wire was stretched sideways down the doline, glittering in the sunlight. Slight clouds dotted the sky, and the sheep, browsing up above on the cliffs, looked like clouds, too. Everything radiated light and life, and it was odd to be thinking about the subterranean world.

"The safety cord," Cosyns ordered, from beneath the tarpaulin where he sat in front of the winch. And Norbert Casteret, with a shade of malice in his old shepherd's face, set about roping off the doline with a long cord, over which the journalists and other onlookers at once unconcernedly stepped.

Coming up from Sainte-Engrâce that morning, my mother had picked a few sprigs of wild pink. She handed them to Loubens, who pinned them to his breast, murmuring with a smile that was not put on for the photographers: "Kiss my son for me."

During this first test, Loubens's task was to place a *diabolo,* which was a sort of large pulley, at a place we had marked the year before −262 feet down, where the suspension cable had cut into the rock and dug a groove nearly a centimeter deep. As the electric motor was not yet connected, the winch was worked by hand with the aid of two great handles, each turned by one man.

The machinery came through the test with flying colors. And so did Loubens, although he had spent five hours in the shaft, digging out with a graver the four holes in the limestone wall in which the spikes for holding the *diabolo* were to be driven. When he came back to the top, he was not in the least exhausted—no staring eyes, or widely dilated pupils, that usually distinguish men who have issued from the dark.

"It's hard, that rock," his Toulouse accent rang out happily. "And what a lot of water there is this year. I could hear the waterfall at −295; last year it was at −490."

Everything had gone well, except for two short hitches on the winch, one going down and the other coming up. These had been quickly dealt with, and the real descents could begin next morning.

Who would be the first to go down? In my capacity as photographic recorder, I should certainly be the second, for my job was to be at the bottom throughout the whole exploration; I wanted someone to precede me, however, into the first cave, the Lépineux cave, and light a powerful flare, so that as I was spinning in space, during the last 350 feet, I could take pictures of its dreamlike merry-go-round of walls and roofs.

We considered all the members of the team, and once again, among those who possessed all the necessary qualifications, Marcel Loubens was pre-eminent. Delighted with this windfall, he put on his gear, buckled up his pack and went down the rope ladder to the bottom of the doline. A newsreel cameraman took pictures, and the shackle of the cable was fastened to the metal bracket set in the sling of his harness.

"A little more slack, please."

On his head he placed his broad, white helmet, adjusted the earphones attached to it, close to his ears, and hooked round his neck the red patches of the throat-microphone.

"Ready."

He threaded his way through the narrow opening, hanging on by his hands to the jack wedged sideways into the gap, on which the counterblock rested. Then, lowering himself at arm's length, he was at last hanging in space.

"Down a bit."

At the handles, Casteret and Cosyns let out slack.

"Halt."

He was standing upright now on a natural terrace 10 feet below the entrance.

"Pass down the packs."

Jimmy and Mairey had fastened two heavy kitbags, stuffed with equipment, to a mountaineer's rope. One after the other, the big canvas rolls were lowered to Loubens, and we could hear the click of his snap hooks. He undid the slip knots.

"Now, I'm ready. Let go, and *au revoir,* boys."

Silently the cable began to move. Leaning over the dark chasm, which exhaled a raw blast of air, we could see the yellow beam of his lamp growing dimmer and dimmer.

As the winch was being worked by hand, instead of by motor, it took about an hour and a half for him to reach the bottom. But this was accomplished without noteworthy incident. From the bottom he telephoned that he had found last year's equipment exactly as we had left it: a reel of 400 yards of telephone wire, and boxes of chocolate, coffee and solid alcohol.

While the cable was coming up again, I got ready: woolen underclothes, woolen shirt and sweater, trousers, a linen overall and on top of that a waterproof overall. I put on my shoes and the special helmet. My torches were checked, and their batteries renewed. We went down into the doline; the team was in fine form: everything was humming along, and we were going to have a smashing success.

There must have been ten of us, at least, in front of the entrance to the chasm. The cable had almost finished hauling up, and it was time to slip on the harness. A few minutes later, the end of the wire appeared. Jimmy grabbed it, brought it over and snapped it on to the safety hook in my harness.

"Ready!"

From the winch, 35 feet above, came the answer: "Wait a moment."

Then: "There's a little thing to put right."

And so we waited. From this moment onward, my memory has passed through some odd fluctuations, and there are blanks that I cannot fill in. I only remember that at the bottom of the doline, everything went off in an easy atmosphere. Norbert Casteret was as dryly humorous as ever, and Jimmy and Mairey were overflowing with good spirits. About an hour went by. Under my rubber overalls, condensation was forming, and it was far from pleasant. We had no idea what they were

The moment of greatest tension up above. André Mairey is giving urgent instructions over the telephone to the companions of Loubens trying to save him after his fall. Another expedition member secures the tips of the throat-microphone against Mairey's neck. After the accident phone conversations became very difficult. Sound had to travel over 400 yards along wire under bad conditions. Fortunately, those on the bottom were able to hear a little better than those on top. (*Paris-Match*)

Over 1,500 feet below the surface, Loubens—before his tragic accident—pauses at the bank of the underground river. The expedition had enthusiastic hopes of using this stream as a source of generating electric power, and of eventually changing the entire economy of the region. This picture was taken in the Elisabeth Casteret cave. (*H. Tazieff*)

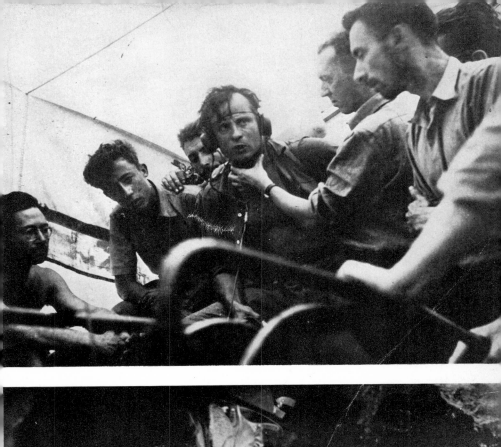
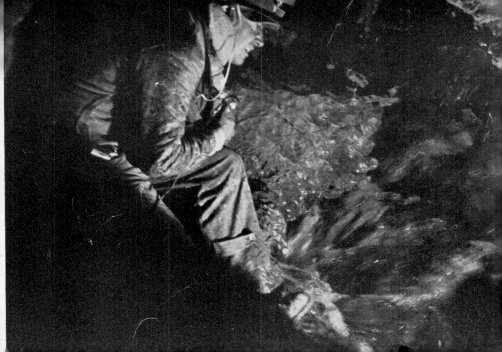

J. Labeyrie is carving the epitaph of his friend Loubens. The dead man had first fallen through 35 feet of empty space, and then ricocheted another 100 feet along the rocky walls of the chasm. The wires of the cable had bitten through their grip and broken. (*Occhialini*)

The epitaph: HERE MARCEL LOUBENS PASSED THE LAST DAYS OF HIS GALLANT LIFE. The task of burying Loubens was long and wearisome. The grave, in the Lépineux cave, was marked by a rough cross made of two squares of sheet metal covered with white luminous paint. (*Labeyrie*) tinkering with on the winch. From the beginning, this piece of machinery had been treated like a sacred relic, and it was no subject for joking.

"Go and see, Casteret," Mairey whispered, "they won't dare to look daggers at you."

A few minutes later Casteret signaled that I might as well undress.

This took place at about 2 P.M., I think, and it was not until 10 P.M. that my descent began. The drum of the winch, on which the wire was coiled, had jammed while being wound up, and the answer to this mishap was not easy to find. Pierre Louis and Max Cosyns worked on it without a pause, and eventually I was able to put on my gear again. Night had fallen, and with it came a fine rain. Only André Treuthard and Jimmy Théodor were still around to lend me a hand. The others had gone to bed, and the effect was rather gloomy.

With no regrets for the dark, damp world, I slipped down to the terrace, and two long heavy kitbags were passed to me by rope. I hooked them on, let go the rope and said farewell to André and Jimmy.

The winch was being worked by Louis and Cosyns, and it was with Cosyns that I was in touch. At the moment of writing these lines, I cannot remember much about my descent. Perhaps I am still too tired, for it is only a month since I came up again, and it has not been a restful month. In front of my eyes passed huge precipitous walls, glistening with damp—there were thousands of feet of shaft, as it seemed. Breaking the smooth, dizzy uniformity here and there was a ledge or a narrow traverse. Now and again limestone sheets, a foot or so wide, bulged out in overhangs, divided from one another by chimneys. The perpendicular tunnel of this chasm sometimes had a circular section 15, 30 or even 40 yards in diameter; sometimes it was very much narrower. It looked like a fracture tremendously enlarged, on one side bounded by a vertical wedge narrowing into impenetrable darkness, and on the other cut off clean by an abrupt wall, absolutely smooth. When the tunnel narrowed, I could see the rock close at hand in the light of my lamp; then it would suddenly widen again, seeming to dissolve into darkness.

Just after the halfway mark came the waterfall. In spite of what Loubens had said, it was no bigger than in 1951. It is best pictured as a tap, fully turned on, producing a heavy, irregular shower that would make one feel like a drowning man fished out of the Seine, were it not for waterproof overalls. Luckily, I was well protected.

It was midnight, and I was pretty tired when my hands

and feet lost touch with the sides of the shaft; I had reached the last 350 feet and was hanging in open space. I began to spin, and depressingly far off, a few minutes later, I saw Loubens's lamp.

"Hi, Marcel, what a devil of a long way!"

"Haroun! You've taken your time! Shall I light the flares?"

I hesitated a moment.

"No. I'm too tired. I haven't the strength to get out the camera. We can do it again in a few days' time; I'll have myself hauled up 200 feet or so."

Then, talking to the surface, I asked: "Did you hear that, Max? Is that all right with you?"

"Yes, yes, that's fine."

But these pictures were fated never to be taken.

After stumbling over great heaps of rubble, carrying our equipment, down to the platform marked out by Loubens, we set up the tent, and about one o'clock in the morning, tottering with fatigue, slipped into our sleeping bags.

IV

Reconnaissances

Two days later, Marcel Loubens and I were laboriously climbing up the last few yards of the steep rubble slope that led to our camp. We had had a hard day. From nine in the morning till seven at night we had been surveying, yard by yard, the extent of the huge cavern discovered in the previous year, and named by Loubens after Elisabeth Casteret. Patiently we had been looking for a pothole, through which we might climb down into a network of caves and galleries yet unexplored. Our lamps probed, and probed again, into walls and corners. Our ears were cocked to catch the distant rumbling of subterranean waters. Even our skin seemed to be on the alert for possible drafts from a vent that would lead still lower.

Very slowly, we went forward, climbing over rocks as high as houses. The lamp, hanging from my neck, lit up peaks, plains and crevices. Looking into the dark, from the top of a pile of rocks, we would plunge down, taking care not to twist our ankles or bark our shins. Now and again, one of us would switch on a long-distance torch,

115

and a beam of light would sweep the darkness, revealing sheer walls, roofs jutting down from nowhere and a chaos of tangled boulders.

Our prospecting had been disappointing; nowhere was there a shaft or a passage leading to lower depths. Only in the roof had we noticed two or three skylights which probably opened into neighboring caves. We had also tried to follow the river, or rather the stream, which threaded its way between the huge boulders heaped up on the bottom of the cave. But again we came to a dead end; the water disappeared into a siphon, so narrow that diving was impossible. The shingle beach that Marcel, in his exhaustion, had thought he had seen last year simply did not exist; in the whole of the cave there was no good camping site.

It was very nearly 7 P.M. when at last we hit upon the entrance to a shaft—to be exact, it was just before the time that had been fixed for us to get in touch with the surface. The stones that we threw down clattered and ricocheted for several seconds, giving off an echo that suggested considerable depth. Fixing a ladder, and setting off down it, would have been easy, but it was late, and in spite of this encouraging find, our spirits were low.

"The best part of this trip," I exclaimed, "will be the articles we'll write. I wonder what I shall say."

Our camp was in the first cave, about 1,250 feet deep, sited on a small terrace, 13 feet square; it was one of the few horizontal slabs in a place where everything sloped away at an angle of 40 degrees. Loubens slept alone in a "Narvik" tent; my own big camp bed could not be accommodated in it. The day before yesterday, we had not gone to bed till two in the morning. And yesterday we had not been much earlier. We had spent almost the whole day dealing with telephone calls, looking after the descent and ascent of André Treuthard, who brought us 130 pounds of equipment, and waiting for a long time, while the lines were blocked, for Jacques Labeyrie to come down. He was the third member of the advance party, and today he had been in charge of all telephone and cable connections.

After we had climbed the ladder, and stumbled over a few yards of rubble, we found Labeyrie in camp; with him was Beppo Occhialini who had just come down from the top. While Jacques was cooking lentils on our gas stove, without the help of fat—for that had been omitted from our stock of provisions—Loubens and I described our finds, watching the light of enthusiasm kindle on Occhialini's features. Any conversation with Beppo soon drifts on to philosophical themes, and it was again the early hours of the morning before we went to bed. We slipped into our sleeping bags, two of us in the tent, and Labeyrie and I outside. Jacques began to whistle an air from a concerto of Vivaldi's, and I fell asleep.

Next morning we scarcely had the heart to climb out of our warm, down bags, put on our damp clothes, and boil the breakfast water. It was late when we set off for the bottom, heavily laden. The others were carrying 110 pounds of fluorescine, and I had 45 pounds of photographic equipment.

Briskly we ran down the flexible metal ladder, 65 feet long, which we had set up the night before, leading to the Elisabeth Casteret cave. Soon we were making our way between huge boulders toward the bed of the stream. Fluorescine colors water so intensely that it can be detected even when it has been very heavily diluted; with its aid we hoped that our underground waters would be identifiable at the place where they came out into the open. One of the basic unknowns in our speleological problem was exactly where Loubens's river issued forth.

We rolled several 20-pound tins down to the bottom of a sort of rocky funnel, 4 or 5 yards wide, where for a short distance the waters flowed in the open. With a turn of his screw driver, Jacques opened the tins, upended them and plunged them into the water sharply, so that the fine red powder would not spread about in the air and make it hard to breathe. In artificial light, fluorescine is a rich vermilion red; when dissolved, it dyes the water a deep emerald. It was a remarkable spectacle to see two men straddled across the stream, handling the white tins with bright red hands, while below them the green waters rushed downstream and disappeared beneath the limestone boulders.

"This is the time for color photography," Loubens said.

I lit a flare, focused my Leica, and then saw that the shutter was not working. Four days of damp had been enough to put my old travel-stained camera out of action.

At six in the evening, while Occhialini and I were putting our equipment in order, the other two carried out a reconnaissance of a fracture we had noticed in the afternoon, where it seemed there might be a dark crevice. Half an hour later, they came back with good news: the cleft was large enough to slip into. It went down several yards into the rock and then took a right-angled turn to the right. Up to then, they had been walking on the level, but now the ground suddenly rose up, and they were halted by the edge of a bluff that fell away into the darkness below them.

"We had no rope with which to make a test, but we thought we saw a chance of climbing into the chasm by coming back toward the cave and circling around the boulder that is separated from the main rock by this fracture."

They were right. They had found the opening; it led to a wide corridor of rubble running steeply down. Eventually they had reached a point, 350 feet lower, where the noise of waters could clearly be heard. This meant that the siphon we had discovered could be by-passed, and the course of the river picked up again.

And there was more to it than that: the place where they had halted seemed to be the entrance to an unknown cave, to which Loubens, in his optimism, attributed huge proportions. Labeyrie, more cautiously, admitted that it might be medium-sized. Whatever it was, the new prospects opening before us were extremely tempting; only fatigue and the lateness of the hour persuaded us to put off the expedition until tomorrow.

"As for me," Loubens said, "I've had my share of fun. I'll go up tomorrow morning. Someone else can take my place."

We should certainly miss Marcel when he was back in the world of light. That evening we all basked in his happy humor. The four of us were in fine spirits, glad to be together and looking forward to fresh discoveries. After a fairly substantial meal of spaghetti with tomatoes, sardines, malt extract and half-moldy bread, we had our first thoroughly good night's sleep.

Except for Beppo, whom we left to sleep on, we got up at eight o'clock. The three of us climbed to the little terrace where the end of the cable was waiting, firmly anchored down. We helped Loubens into his kit: waterproofs, strong helmet, parachute harness, bags of equipment slung from its hooks, safety lamp and throat-microphone. Once more there was that curious conversation with the surface, in which listeners must guess the questions, for they can only hear the answers.

"Hello, surface. I'm ready."

". . . ."

"Go ahead," Loubens answered.

Happy anticipation lent a trembling note to his voice.

Slowly the cable stretched taut, running diagonally from the camp where we were standing up to the black square window, formed by the lower end of the shaft, and lit up against the smooth slab of the cave's ceiling in the powerful beam of my torch. Step by step, Loubens mounted the slope, looking like a puppet on the end of his wire, with his kitbags dragging behind him over the pebbles and sharp rocks. Alongside him, Labeyrie and I climbed over the boulders, skidding on rolling stones.

"Don't forget, Marcel, to tell them what we want

urgently: olive oil, concentrated soup, meat and ham, acetylene lamps and bread, if there is any."

"And if you haven't changed your minds since last night, I'll send you down all the girls from the Hotel Bouchet. . . . No, nothing," he told the throat-microphone, "I was talking to the men down here."

A few steps farther and the cable stopped.

"Hello? What's going on?"

". . . ."

"A hitch on the winch? Will it take long?"

". . . ."

"Five minutes? O.K."

All three of us sat down on the damp rocks, and patiently waited. A quarter of an hour went by, and then half an hour. There's a lot of waiting in potholing—it's all part of the game. Sometimes one has to wait in uncomfortable and even dangerous positions, but this time it was easy; we were peacefully installed in damp, rocky armchairs.

"I should have stayed another day at the bottom," Loubens remarked with a shade of regret in his voice. "Whatever you say, Jacques, I think that cave is really tremendous." And he rolled the "r," drawing the word out in all its syllables.

"Perhaps you're right," Labeyrie answered, "but we saw nothing conclusive."

Labeyrie had all the Cartesian caution appropriate to the man of science that he is. "Let's keep our sense of proportion," he went on. "We must be methodical; otherwise we'll get no results."

"But I could *feel* the size of that cave."

For a moment Jacques was deep in thought.

"You could be right. You have a feeling for caves; you can certainly sense them better than we do."

A feeling for caves is very much like a feeling for mountains, for the desert or the sea. It may be an innate gift, but this intuitive sense is certainly sharpened by long habit, accumulated experience and a mind trained in observation. From the age of seventeen to twenty-nine, Marcel Loubens had been exploring one cave and pothole after another, under the wise direction and guidance of the most knowledgeable of speleologists—Norbert Casteret.

"Yes," Loubens went on, "I think that the cave goes a long way. I shouldn't be surprised if there was much more stream in it than what we've found so far."

"In terms of kilowatts, that'll be something," I said.

"Rather."

On the evening before, Labeyrie had suddenly burst

into enthusiasm when we were approaching the stream where the fluorescine was to be dissolved.

"I say. This is fantastic!"

"What?"

"At a yard to the second, with a breadth of 2 yards, and a depth of—let's say 50 yards on the average. That would make . . ." And a rapid succession of figures had followed, uttered in Labeyrie's characteristically clear and precise tone of voice. ". . . Thirty million cubic yards a year at the least. In fact, the figure is higher, for it's low water now, as you can see from the level of the clay several yards above us. If the output were regulated, and in this kind of cave there'd be no wizardry in that, one could count on 100 million cubic yards, at least."

Labeyrie had paused, looking keenly into our faces, his eyes sparkling with a technician's enthusiasm.

"The next thing would be to drive a tunnel, a horizontal gallery starting from the mountainside. It needn't be very long, 200 yards perhaps."

"Three hundred," I added cautiously.

"All right, 300. Driving it horizontally, the Soum de Lèche precipice can be by-passed. The slope is steep from there on, and we can't be far from it. Three hundred yards, at 1 million to the yard, makes 300 millions. As soon as it runs out, the water could be channeled and sent rushing down to Licq or Arette in the valley."

"It would be Arette," Loubens said.

"Very well, Arette. Altitude here is about 4,000 feet, and, as Arette must be 1,650, there would be a fall of 2,350. Turn that into kilowatts for me, my dear sir, and reckon them in devalued francs!"

We checked our mathematics. And though our calculations may have been approximate, we carefully kept optimism out of them. The cost of the tunnel, channel and hydroelectric station could be paid off in four years. After that, there would be sheer profit.

"After all," Labeyrie wound up, gilding the lily, "they often undertake far bigger works for much less important reasons. Take Tré-la-Tête, for example; there, they've dug out over a mile of galleries in order to fetch water from a melting glacier. Ten times as much effort and expense for half or a third of the water there is here. . . ."

V

A brief cry

TIME was passing, and we were still sitting on the damp boulders. What could be going on up above? It had been like this since Loubens had first come down, five days ago. Nobody ever told the men at the bottom exactly what was happening: why the cable had stopped, or why there was no reply on the telephone.

"It's like being in the front line, and grousing about the men in the rear," Loubens said.

"I bet the men on top grouse about us."

"It's fair enough. There are bound to be gripes when we can't talk to one another, or say clearly what we mean."

"But we're not in a bed of roses here, and if something's gone wrong with the winch, they might tell us what it is. And how long it will take to fix it."

"They may think it would worry us."

Labeyrie was trying to set our minds at rest.

"Worry us? But we're not children. Either the break-down can be repaired in a given time, and then we're off,

126

or it can't. If it can't, there's nothing to get flustered about. We should only have to wait for them to fetch another winch, or lower ladders down the shaft."

I got up to stretch my legs and warm myself. Labeyrie did likewise. Loubens, huddled in his armor, had to stay still. Imprisoned in his heavy accouterments, he was almost as incapable of movement of his own accord as a man in a diving suit out of the water.

A few steps away, Labeyrie set his camera and took a picture of the dark motionless statue of a man equipped, so it seemed, for some interplanetary journey, lit up in the total darkness only by the beam of his breast lamp. Coming nearer, he took a close up, under the helmet, of Loubens's determined features. At that moment, word came from the surface that all was in order and the ascent could begin.

"Good-by. Have a good trip. Regards to all on top. Make them send us some reinforcements. Tell them there can never be too many people on this sort of job."

Once more the cable stretched taut. Over the rubble, and from boulder to boulder, Loubens set off on his slow progress, looking strangely as if he were no longer subject to the laws of gravity.

He held in his left hand a sort of thick stick, not 2 feet long. It was his magnesium torch, and, when he had been hoisted up a few yards, he was to light it. In its vivid glare, I was to take pictures of the extraordinary sight of a man hanging in space, being slowly hauled up to the square hole in the ceiling through which he would disappear.

Jacques Labeyrie halted, setting his camera where he stood. I climbed up higher, on Loubens's heels; and when he began to be hauled over the big smooth boulder that crowned the rubble slope, I stepped to the left in order to get a good view.

This was it: Loubens was taking off. Ten yards ahead of me, in the beam of my lamp, I could make out his shadowy silhouette, rising slowly, and spinning on the end of the cable. I wanted to record this impressive circling motion on film, and we were determined not to let Loubens off lightly. It was our practice, however, always to try to reduce this disagreeable eddying motion for anyone going up or coming down, by keeping tautly stretched the telephone wire that connected with the departure terrace at the bottom. This was not merely a friendly gesture, for after an ascent had been made, the real purpose of the wire was to allow the steel cable, which ended in an aluminum shell containing the hook and the telephone plugs, to be guided down again through space without risk of catching in a trap of the rock.

Loubens had now gone up 35 feet. There was a halt. The cable stopped; a match crackled, flaming astonishingly bright in the darkness, and then went out. Loubens was revolving, and I could see the yellowish disc of his breast lamp flashing on and off like the beam of a tiny lighthouse. A second match flared and a third. At any moment I was expecting to be dazzled by the radiance of magnesium, but it did not catch.

"I can't light it," Loubens shouted. "I'm in an air stream, and there's too much draft."

After a moment's silence, I could hear him saying to the surface: "No, I was talking to Tazieff."

I raised my camera to eye level; in the view finder I could clearly see the beam of Loubens's lamp as it flashed and vanished. Its coming and going might take on film— one never knows—and the effect would be terrific; I pressed the knob, and the camera softly whirred.

The magnesium flare still refused to catch. Only the little lighthouse beam was spinning, one flash per second. I stopped shooting, but kept the camera glued to my eye, with my finger on the knob, ready to shoot again.

There was a brief cry of distress. In deep silence, I watched the beam of the lamp dart down the shaft. A fraction of a second later, the sound of crashing filled

my ears. Three steps away, Loubens's body rolled clattering past me.

The thing had happened which we had always refused
to believe, always held to be utterly impossible. Often
enough, after last year's expedition, and before we had
set off on this, people had said to us: "But aren't you
afraid when you hang in space, 1,300 feet down, on the
end of a wire that's only a few millimeters thick?" Of
course, we should have been terror-stricken, if we had
let our imaginations dwell on the thinness of wires, the
slenderness of spindles and the breakability of split pins.
But does anyone taking an airplane stop to consider possible flaws in the propeller shaft?

So there it was. We had been betrayed by the machine
in which we had placed our trust; the machine that had
been designed, blueprinted and specially built for us.

After falling 35 feet through space, and, for another
100 feet, rolling and ricocheting from rock to rock,
Loubens's body came to rest in an unconscious heap.
Labeyrie had reached him and put an end to his frightful
fall by holding him back upon the rubble.

Moving cautiously, so as not to send stones clattering
down upon my friends, and to avoid the risk of a second
accident, I climbed down the 50 or 60 feet of rock and
stones.

VI

Loubens's life hung on the turn of a screw

LOUBENS was lying flat on his stomach across the slope, his head turned slightly to one side. Anxiously I flashed my lamp over his face, stained with blood flowing from his mouth and nose. No blood seemed to be issuing from his ears.

"Perhaps he hasn't fractured his skull?"

Clinging to this ray of hope, and praying for a miracle, we shouted to Occhialini, who was still asleep down below in the tent. "Hi, Beppo!" we cried, and then Labeyrie roared, "Help, help!" to make Beppo understand at once that something terrible had happened. I added my voice to his.

One never shouts for help unless one is crushed and overwhelmed by a force against which it is impossible to struggle alone. Asking others for aid is a confession of impotence, an entreaty for compassion, a kind of self-renunciation. This shattering catastrophe had, indeed, overwhelmed us.

Occhialini came up panting after climbing the steep

slope at too rapid a pace. He had not even given himself time to put on his boots, but rushed toward us, scrambling across the damp and icy stones. He was carrying Labeyrie's sleeping bag and camp bed.

"We must turn him over on to his back," I suggested.

"Take care. If his spinal column is broken, we oughtn't to touch him."

"But we must move him. We can't leave him here under the fall of stones from the shaft."

Puzzled and lost in thought, Occhialini bit his lips.

"I'm going to get some canvas," he announced suddenly, and ran down the slope in his stocking feet.

Standing on the cave side of the body, we propped it up with our whole weight, anxious to prevent Loubens from toppling down the overhang on which he rested, and starting his sickening fall all over again. He was breathing in quick, deep gasps, horribly like the bellows of a forge. He had lost his spectacles, and I looked into his half-closed eyes, with two contradictory hopes in mind: that his eyes would open and he would tell us, "I am going to live," or that they would shut tight, showing that he was unconscious and unable to feel the pain he must be suffering.

Beppo came back with the canvas. He had still not

stopped to put on his boots, and I scolded him: "You'll catch pneumonia, and that'll be a lot of help to us."

Crinkling his eyes, he shook his head, very much the Italian, and sighed: "Ah! . . ."

Turning Loubens over gave us a lot of trouble. He was a big man, and terribly heavy. We slipped him into the canvas, doing our best to combine gentleness in handling with the need to keep our balance. Then we bore him, a foot at a time, to the only place relatively sheltered from the fall of stones where he could lie flat— the site of our old camp. It was only a matter of 20 yards but it took us half an hour. We stretched Loubens on his camp bed and covered him with the sleeping bag. With both hands I grasped the ear pieces of his helmet and pulled them as far apart as they would go. Labeyrie lifted his head, and I took the helmet off. We examined his skull anxiously, but there seemed to be nothing abnormal. On the surface of the helmet, in the substance of the spun glass laid bare where the paint had been scratched away, two stars spread out, indicating the points at which he had crashed. After a clear fall of 35 feet, the glass helmet had stood up well; had it been made of steel, it would certainly have been staved in.

"I'm going to see if I can find the end of the cable," Labeyrie said.

I had been thinking of that. If it had occurred to them to let it down again, we would be able to telephone. Striding off calmly, Labeyrie vanished into the night. Occhialini and I were silent; the only sounds were of pebbles rolling down the slope, and the quick noisy breathing of the man lying at our knees.

Labeyrie came back with the cable. They must have realized on top that something unusual had happened, and they had let out slack. Labeyrie had found the wire lying in loose coils between the boulders at the top of the cave. He was holding in his hand the aluminum shell, designed to protect the hook from shocks. He came up without saying a word; looking at us with a melancholy set expression, he handed over the shell. The cable entered it through the hole bored in the head, as was normal. But it was far from normal at the other end; there was no shackle, 2 inches long by 1 inch wide, into which the hook, attached to the harness straps, ought to have been snapped; instead, a tangle of frayed steel threads hung out, and mixed in with them the red-copper core of the telephone wire, looking gilded inside its transparent plastic sheath.

I gazed, bewildered, utterly unable to fathom the meaning of this spray of metal threads, which should have been clamped together with a little ring and a nut.

"What happened?"

In precise technical language, Labeyrie explained. "The clamp has proved inadequate for long service. Due to constant vibration, and contraction caused by the cold, the wire has bitten through the cable grip."

It is terrible to think that a man's life should depend on a little steel ring and the turn of a screw. A man's life that had comprised thirty years of work, struggle, worry, tribulation and love. All this was snuffed out for want of a pin, or an extra turn of a spanner.

Labeyrie connected the earphones and adjusted the throat-microphone.

"Hello, the winch! Hello, the winch!"

". . . ."

"Labeyrie here. Loubens has had a fall, about an hour ago. He is badly hurt."

He waited for an answer, then said: "Put him on."

Speaking lower, he added to us: "They're putting me over to Mairey."

Mairey was one of the best men on the team, and the expedition's doctor.

There was a pause.

"Mairey? Hello!"

". . . ."

"Yes, he's been unconscious ever since."

". . . ."

"His breathing is quick, fifty-eight exhalations to the minute. There's some slaver; it froths and bubbles. Fracture of the upper jaw, and something at the hips; he keeps trying to put his right hand on it."

". . . ."

"I can't hear. Please repeat."

". . . ."

"I still can't hear."

". . . ."

"Keep him motionless?"

". . . ."

"Say it again."

". . . ."

"Keep him motionless on a flat, steady surface? All right."

". . . ."

"And you'll come down as fast as possible? Excellent. We'll be seeing you. Put me over to Lévi."

There was a silence, while up above they changed earphones and throat-microphones. Then talk started again, though all we could hear of it was the short, sharp remarks of Labeyrie.

"Hello, Robert."

". . . ."

"Fix ladders in the shaft?"

Jacques looked at us inquiringly. We all had the same reaction: it could not be done, and it was easy to see that they did not understand the position.

Labeyrie explained: "No; ladders are out of the question. Marcel is too exposed; his legs and pelvis can't be protected from showers of stones. If you start driving in spikes and fixing ladders, tons of roughcast will come down. It's nine to ten that Marcel would be hit."

". . . ."

"Yes, the best thing is to send down Mairey as fast as you can."

". . . ."

"Yes, haul up the cable, and mend the broken shackle. Then send the doctor down. Good-by."

And so our wait began.

VII

In the dark with a dying man

IT MUST have been about noon. The cable began to go
up, and I was keeping watch on the uncoiling telephone
wire, which we had fastened to the bottom of the cable
shell. When the winch was carrying no load, it took only
an hour to haul the cable in. But suddenly the drum
stopped. Jacques picked up the earphones and I took his
place at Marcel's bedside.

Communication was difficult: sounds had to travel
over 400 yards of cable, and then over 400 yards of
wire. It was a long way. This time Labeyrie could hear
distinctly what was said to him, but the men on top could
not hear him.

"They tell me they're repairing the cable lug. Pierre
Louis is working on it, non-stop. He's using reinforced
clamping screws. The whole country has been given the
alarm. The broadcasting people arrived at the winch as
soon as the news was known. A helicopter is on its way;
it left Germany this morning."

"Germany? Why Germany?"

138

"I've no idea. In any case, I'm not sure whether they said Germany or England. There's an ambulance airplane as well, and potholing teams from various places, like Pau and Mauléon. The five youngsters from Lyons, who were down the Fertel hole the other day, have also turned up. They had gone down to see where the fluorescine came out."

A warm feeling of gratitude filled us for the help that was spontaneously coming to Loubens from all parts of the country. But, in the meantime, we felt horribly impotent; there was nothing we could do to assist Loubens in his heroic struggle with death. For that was what he was undergoing; the tremendous expense of energy, manifested in his furious breathing, was a sign of the pitiless struggle of life against death. I had a feeling that death was a beast of prey, unrelentingly patient, lurking behind one of the walls of rock and needing to make no special effort to accomplish its fell purpose. Death has no battle to win or lose. It is always with us, and it is life that does the fighting. Inexorably this was borne in upon me as we waited in the dark, damp cave, echoing with the panting breath of an unconscious man.

"Let's hope Mairey gets here before he regains consciousness," I said.

"Yes, it would be frightful if . . ."

I was frozen with horror at the idea of Marcel's coming to, and being in agony with the pain of his shattered body. For his sake and ours, since we were wholly unable to ease his sufferings, I hoped that the effects of shock would last until the doctor had come down with his sedatives.

But hours went by, and still the cable was under repair. Mairey could not come down, and Loubens fought on without weakening.

"A man's pretty tough, when you come to consider . . ."

"But what a lot of energy he's losing every hour, breathing like that," said Jacques. "Ought we to try to make him swallow a drop of coffee or milk?"

"How can we? His throat's congested with mucus. We might choke him if we tried liquids."

"Perhaps we should put a hot-water bottle on his chest. That would restore a few calories."

I climbed down to the camp to light the stove, while Occhialini went off to find water. There was relatively little in the cave, for the streamlets were inaccessibly hidden under the heaps of rubble that cluttered the bottom. Because of this, we had been obliged to collect our water supplies, literally drop by drop. The best place lay 20 yards away from the camp, immediately underneath the little overhang where Loubens's fall had been halted. It took half an hour's patient work to collect a quart of water. Occhialini came back, boiled a billycan, filled a flask and placed it under the sleeping bag on the injured man's chest.

From the top we had had little news, for the transmission was getting worse. Jacques was tireless in trying to maintain contact, sometimes by voice and sometimes in Morse, using one of the telephone wires as a sending key. But he was not very successful. Then things improved, and though the surface could hardly hear us, we could understand them.

"It's Jimmy speaking," Jacques reported. "He says they're still working on the cable hook. The police have brought up a radio set to keep in touch with the valley. Norbert Casteret has warned Loubens's parents."

My heart bled for his poor parents. It must have been frightful for them to know that their son was in danger of death, and to be utterly powerless to help him. Only 400 yards separated our friend's sickbed from the possibility of recovery. But these 400 yards were as hard to cross as a desert or an ocean.

"Have they told Huguette?"

Jacques passed the question on through the throat-

Holding the cable taut to support Tazieff while the winch is being repaired. The men are down at the bottom of the doline by the cave entrance, the winch is out of sight above. Among the first to come to assistance was the author's father. He and his wife had hurried to the scene at the first news of the disaster. The repair of the winch occupied an interminable time, during which Tazieff was suspended in the void underneath a waterfall. Great care had to be taken by the men to avoid any jerk that might have snapped the wire. (*M. Descamps for Paris-Match*)

Tazieff's mother awaits the return of her son, then suspended under the waterfall. She and her husband had been living in the camp for several days, along with reporters, shepherds and gendarmes, ever since news of the ascents had reached the world. Mme. Tazieff sent a message to her son: "Tell him . . . to be patient, and that I'm here; I bring people luck." (*Paris-Match*)

The author after he finally reached the surface. Absolute exhaustion had overcome him on the way up. The last man to return was Dr. André Mairey—his final night below the earth was spent beside the body of the man who gave his life for the expedition, Marcel Loubens. (*France-Soir*, SCOOP) microphone, but Jimmy could not catch it. Eventually, he got it through to the top by Morse.

"Yes, and she's taken it bravely."

Jacques went on relaying to us whatever words he could catch. "They are full of anxiety on top. A great deal more so than we are. Probably because they're not so closely involved."

About 5 P.M., the wires went dead.

"The circuit is still working," Labeyrie declared. "What can be going on?"

For over an hour, he did everything he could to get in touch again. But all was silent on top. Gradually, at the bottom of the chasm, we began to feel that we had been left to our fate; for we were just as incapable of bringing out our friend, or climbing out ourselves, as if we had been corked up in a gigantic black bottle.

"The bastards! What on earth can they be doing?"

I no longer dared glance at my watch; the hands were moving too slowly. A mere five minutes had laboriously gone by since I had last looked. It was 8 P.M., and then 8:30. Marcel was still gasping, and in the same frenetic rhythm. Mucous foam was now coming out of his nostrils as well as from his mouth. Now and again, one of us leaned over him to wipe his lips with a damp cloth.

"We ought to have something to eat. It's no time to run down our strength."

"What shall we have?"

I rummaged among the few boxes lying between the boulders. "Well, there are sardines, biscuits, Nescafé and sugar."

Food and a hot drink did us good. Nine P.M. came round, and we were still out of touch with the top. We decided to take turns resting in the camp down below, and I went off duty first.

VIII

Has he a chance, Doctor?

WHEN I woke, both fingers of my watch were pointing to twelve. For an instant I was puzzled: was it noon or midnight? But I was still far too sleepy for it to be as late as noon.

I had undressed before slipping into my sleeping bag. Whether one is in the mountains, at sea or under the earth, sleep is always more refreshing if one has a change of clothes. Now I needed to summon all my strength in order to get out of the soft, dry warmth of the bag, and put on my soaking trousers, damp shoes, and overalls.

I had slept in the tent, on one of our rubber mattresses. When I had entered this little lair, I had not stopped to wonder why I was exchanging my own camp bed for a rubber mattress that I normally detested. But as soon as I opened the tent's narrow circular entrance, I knew why I had avoided my own big bed that lay outside. The terrible, huge darkness of the cave surrounded me, and Loubens's gasps echoed in the air, reminding me of the pain he was suffering and our impotence to help him. For three hours of troubled sleep I had escaped from this nightmare. Now I had to open eyes and ears to hard reality.

I joined my friends up at the old camp site. They had managed to settle down with the minimum of discomfort, squatting on a rubber mattress at Loubens's bedside, covering their legs with tent canvas against the penetrating cold. They had spent the last three hours collecting water, wiping Marcel's mouth and vainly trying to re-establish contact with the surface.

I took Jacques's place, and he went off to sleep. The night drew on endlessly, heavy with our anxious silence, and echoing with Loubens's bellows-like breathing. Now and again I put on the earphones and connected the throat-microphone.

"Hello, winch! Hello, winch! Tazieff here."

There was no reply, not even the faint scratching noise which would have meant that the circuit was shut off.

"What can they be doing? For heaven's sake, do you suppose they've all run away?"

"Tell me," Occhialini suddenly asked, "how did the Spaniards behave when they came along the other day?"

"What? Do you think those carabiniers have clapped everyone in jail? Nonsense! Besides, they were most friendly, and especially the captain."

The captain had indeed been likable; he was a man of about forty, with light chestnut hair and a balding forehead. We had spent two hours together in the hollow of the wild valley near the frontier stone of Pierre Saint-Martin. Four Spaniards had paid this duty call, and they had waited patiently while our official letters were copied out, certifying that our party was not engaged in espionage. Two of us had gone to meet them—Marcel, who spoke Spanish well, and myself to take pictures of them.

Loubens and the captain had had an agreeable chat, punctuated by lengthy silences in which the warm breeze could be heard singing in the emerald branches of the pines. They had cracked jokes, and everyone had laughed, including myself, who understood only half of what was said. No: even if we had flagrantly violated the frontier, men like that, who knew that Loubens was in danger of his life down here, would never order the team on top to evacuate at a time when they were doing their utmost, so we hoped, to rescue us.

"The bastards! They might at least give us a sign of life, shake the cable or throw down a stone! They have no idea what it's like to be down here knowing absolutely nothing."

From time to time we straightened Loubens's head, and wiped away the mucus.

"Tazieff!"

"What?"

I had dozed off, but the note of alarm in Occhialini's voice jerked me back to realities.

"The flow from his mouth has stopped. It's only coming from his nose. The poison must be rising in him. What can we do?"

We could do nothing; two sleeping bags, a hot-water bottle and our own anxiety were all we had to offer.

At five in the morning, Labeyrie returned to relieve Occhialini, who took his spell of sleep. New hope rose in me of re-establishing contact, for I had great confidence in Labeyrie's patience and skill. But even the most competent workman can do little at the bottom of a cave when the men on top have shut off the circuit.

"I wish they'd go screw themselves."

Jacques had squatted down beside me, and we were practically hugging one another in an attempt to get warm. More hours went by. Suddenly Jacques nudged me and I looked round. He motioned to the telegraph wire, stretching upward from its drum, and just discernible in the faint light of a carbide lamp. It was waving and shaking. I glanced at my watch: it was 8 A.M.

"So they can't be all dead up there."

At once we jumped up and began to wind in the

wire as it came down. After fifteen hours, it was at last descending. Fifteen hours, in which we had been completely cut off from the world, with no idea of what was happening, and no power to do anything to help a man struggling for his life. The strain had reached a point that is utterly indescribable. And now there was new hope: we knew at last that the world outside still existed and that it was really concerned with rescuing the injured man, though the only evidence we had was the motion of a copper wire.

It was impossible to telephone while someone was suspended on the cable. Very likely it was Mairey, and he alone would be able to talk to the top. His descent seemed to be going smoothly, and as we rolled in the wire, the prospect of saving Loubens grew brighter.

Loubens was still wrestling with death, inhaling and exhaling rhythmically, with the regularity of a machine. It was the machine of life. We started heating up water, so the doctor would find the few preparations we could make all ready for him. In the course of the night, we had filled from the spring all the flasks, billycans and other containers we had. On the low flame of the stove we boiled a 3-quart pressure cooker.

It was indeed André Mairey. At about 9:30 we recognized his voice giving directions to the surface through the throat-microphone. A few minutes later, the small yellow circle of his torch flashed brightly through the shadows. He began to spin in space, and to steady him we pulled on the telephone wire fastened to his belt. Eventually he landed on the big boulder at the top, and slid along the wall, stumbling over the smaller stones and shingle.

The doctor had come down with a Tyrolian rucksack on his back and a metal stretcher attached to his harness. We helped him to find his footing, unharness himself and take off the helmet that was pinching his ears. I do not recall what we said, but I remember how delighted Labeyrie and I were to see his fine, broad face shining with good will. We shook hands over and over again. Then Mairey bent over the injured man, while we watched him anxiously. He pulled a face and shook his head.

"Has he a chance, Doc?"

"No. He's done for."

I believe I shall never forget those three words, spoken softly in the lilting accent of Franche-Comté, which always reminds me of my own Liége: "He's done for."

"But why? The skull's not broken."

"Oh, yes. Fractured skull and fractured spinal column."

"But he could move his legs. At least, he did a little when we were carrying him. And he hasn't bled from the ears."

"He's bled from the nose, and there's no injury there. It's the spinal column, for certain."

With quiet precision, he took out his instruments.

"We'll do what we can. If there's the slightest chance, he shall have it."

I was reluctant to give up hope. It may be wrong to be a natural optimist, but sometimes there are advantages. Desperately I recalled aloud one of my own experiences, when I had fallen a clear 30 feet while climbing among the rocks of the Meuse. I had landed flat on my back on a horizontal slab. Thirty feet was nearly as far as Loubens had dropped, and I had only suffered a gash in the elbow and a bruised backside.

"Maybe," said Mairey, "but this is more serious."

IX

Attempting the impossible

MAIREY set to work in earnest concentration. He broke ampoules, filled syringes and gave injections. Without looking, I knew what he was doing.

Confronted by our struggling friend, and by our own impotence to get him out of the trap we were in, we had gradually accumulated a feeling almost of guilt. The longer the incomprehensible silence had lasted on top, and the longer the rescue had been delayed, Loubens's chances had steadily diminished, and on our shoulders had rested the heavy responsibility of keeping him alive. But what could the three of us do about it? Nothing but wipe his mouth, straighten his head and keep him warm.

Now the doctor was here, the responsibility was no longer ours. But I felt no relief; I was too stupefied and exhausted. Mairey diagnosed an open fracture of the left shoulder.

"It will be best to put it in plaster before moving him."

Occhialini had joined us, after five hours of broken sleep, induced by sleeping tablets. He had been tired

155

when he had arrived from Brazil, and though he had only been underground four days, he looked all in; his jaw jutted out, his face was emaciated and his eyes were sunken.

"Mairey," he said in his high-pitched voice, "if something has to be done, let me do it, because I'm not sure how long I can last. . . ."

"Yes, his arm needs pulling, the left one. Take him by the wrist and tug with all your might."

Occhialini grasped Marcel's limp wrist. He bit his lips and shut his eyes—or, rather, clamped his eyelids together just as fiercely as he bit his lips. Then he began to pull.

While at work, André told us what had been going on up above.

"It was a terrible blow for us on top."

"And for us," said Labeyrie.

"I wanted to come down at once."

"Yes, so you told us, and how we hoped you would."

"My dear fellow, I was seething with impatience. But that cable lug took an age to repair. I assure you it won't break again!"

"I hope not!"

"Then there was the parachute drop about five o'clock yesterday evening. . . ."

"Five o'clock," I put in, "but that was when we lost contact."

"Of course. As soon as the aircraft began circling, everyone rushed off to make signals to it."

"The bastards. Why didn't they let us know?"

"Yes, you'd have thought some saving miracle was going to be dropped to them out of that machine. . . ."

"Straight from heaven," Labeyrie added.

"Well, it was a wonderful sight to see the big three-engined craft circling in the stormy, red and dark gray twilight."

He was making good progress with the plaster cast. It was a relief to see the dislocated limb turning into a neat and clean white cylinder.

"Was the drop far off?"

"Yes, there was a devil of a wind, and the parachutes were carried away down to the edge of the forest."

"Good heavens! That would make a long trip. Who fetched the containers?"

"Oh, there was no lack of volunteers. The police, the shepherds, the boys from Mauléon and Pau and the local lads in Licq and Arette."

"Were the two Bouchets there?"

"I should say so! They took on one of the loads."

"But after the parachute drop, why wasn't contact renewed?"

"I don't know. All I can say is that something clogged up the throat-microphone and, after the parachuting, they set about mending it."

"I can tell you, it's no fun to be left down here without knowing what's happening."

André looked at his questioner without answering; he merely nodded his head in agreement.

"What then?"

"Night fell, and there was a frightful storm. Really frightful. It blew away the winch tent. We had everything—rain, lightning and wind at gale force. In those conditions, we could not consider managing a descent— at least, not without serious risks. And so I had to wait till morning."

"Couldn't he be nursed down here?" asked Occhialini, who had not spoken for some time.

"Down here? It's impossible. With what he's got, he needs absolutely ideal conditions to stand even the ghost of a chance of pulling through. And look at the conditions down here!"

"But you told us not to move him, so as not to cause lesions in the spinal marrow."

"Yes, but there's no chance of saving him if we don't

take him up. He will have to be strapped tightly to the stretcher so as to lessen the risks of lesions. It's going to be tough, very tough."

Suddenly we heard in the distance a noise that our trained ears recognized at once: falling stones. A pebble was clattering down the long perpendicular shaft, rebounding from wall to wall. In a concerted movement, we all crouched down, with arms folded behind our necks. Our heads met, and touched, a few inches above Loubens's stomach. With the breadth of our backs, we tried to give the lower half of his body as much cover as we could, for it had not been possible to shift the whole of him into the lee of the rock.

With a loud crash, the stone reached the bottom of the shaft and burst into fragments, which shot off, as they usually did, in the direction of the spring, the big pieces whirring and the small ones softly whistling.

We stood up again, and Mairey finished his work on the plaster cast.

"That will be the boys fixing the ladders," he remarked.

"Who are they?"

"The youngsters from Lyons."

"Splendid," cried Beppo. "They're first rate with ladders; I saw them last week coming out of Fertel."

"We shall have to look out for roughcast," Jacques

said. "They'll be letting some loose as they drive in the spikes."

Mairey clicked his teeth; he was tired after his descent, and he had had to carry the weight of the stretcher. His nerves must have been taut to breaking point, though he did not let it appear. He had been the first man to come down these 1,200 feet and more, after Loubens had smashed down to the bottom.

His injections finished, Mairey stood up and looked at his patient. "We must give him some peace for a while. Presently, we can strap him to the stretcher and haul him up, or try to."

"It won't be easy."

"No, it won't. And I'd like to have a nap before we try."

Occhialini went off with him, leading him toward the camp. Labeyrie and I crouched down by Marcel's bedside, huddling together under our piece of canvas.

An exacting job of work began next day. We had to move Loubens from the bed on which he had been lying, since the accident, onto the stretcher. Usually casualties are laid out on a bed of wire netting framed by steel, and this rests on a tubular understructure. Before he had come down, Mairey had adapted the stretcher so that it would be the best possible vehicle for carrying a casualty up an abyss. Instead of placing Loubens on a sort of metal mattress, we had to insert him into the space between the tubular shafts of the stretcher's understructure. First, we put down a layer of sleeping bags, and then we tried to lift our friend onto it. It was very difficult, for there was no good foothold. The slab on which we stood was narrow, and its middle was encumbered by a rock too deeply rooted to pull out. In these conditions, we had a lot of trouble lifting Loubens, who in his kit must have weighed close to 200 pounds; and, in any case, we were exhausted. Besides, we had to take infinite care not to disturb his spinal cord.

It was a long job, but at last we completed it. Then there was another task. It was a matter of fastening Loubens to the parachute harness, which we had taken off the night before, but by which he was now to be hoisted up to the surface. Once this was done, we had to strap him extremely tightly to his stretcher. Lacing a prone man with parachute straps may seem to be no trouble at all. But this man was one of our best friends, and the accident had turned him into a child whom we wanted to protect as might a mother; the slightest false step on our part would have killed him on the spot, and on the rough ground where we were maneuvering there was not even room to place two feet on the same level. Besides, the muscles of our arms and shoulders were utterly exhausted, and it seemed a superhuman task to buckle this panting, unconscious body into a harness that should have been as easy to put on as a waistcoat.

X

The last gasp

DESPERATELY, I hoped that Loubens would be given every chance. I wanted to see him lying in one of those clean, white, shining clinics where there is every miraculous device for preserving the sparks of life in a dying man. But we could not hurry things. We could only drudge on, slowly and carefully, in the flickering light of our lamps.

Once Loubens was on the stretcher, we had to make him fast. It was important to be sure that when the stretcher was hoisted, headfirst, he would not double over on himself. Nor should he slip sideways, if the stretcher happened to bump against the walls of the shaft. The problem was to bind him tight, but not too tight. And then there was the question of his helmet. But Mairey had thought of everything before coming down; he had bored two small holes in a helmet, through which a wire could be passed, so that Marcel's head might be secured to the stretcher, and would not jounce about. He had

163

also prepared a hollowed-out plank, into which the rounded back of the helmet would fit.

André took Loubens's head gently between his hands, and I stretched open the elastic earpads and slipped the helmet on. Loubens was ready to go up. The only thing that remained to do, down below, was to effect a blood transfusion. Meanwhile, up above, we had to wait for the flexible ladders to be put into place across overhands and through bottlenecks, and for men to be stationed on ledges and traverses where they could help the stretcher on its way up. We could hear them at work now—or, rather, we could hear them signaling to one another with whistles, as they toiled perilously in the shaft. It requires a considerable physical effort to lower a ladder perpendicularly for even 350 feet. Here the rescue team had to scatter themselves over a distance of 790 feet; there were two men at −260 feet, a third at −390, a fourth at −590 and the last at −790. They were fixing 65-foot ladder lengths, end to end, and then climbing down one after the other, roped together, as in mountaineering. When they reached a relay station, they drove a spike into a cleft, slung themselves from it with a loop of rope and a snap hook, waited for the next man and secured him, so that he could descend still lower. In spite of their care and skill, now and again they dislodged a loose stone, and we would hear it rebounding down the shaft with a crash, followed by silence, a louder crash, and another silence. With helmets on, we crouched over Loubens's body, ready for the shock. After the final silence, while the stone fell down the last 360 feet of open space, it would come hurtling out into the cave, literally exploding and firing fragments past our ears.

The whistling was getting louder: one blow meant stop; two blows, climb up; three blows, climb down. Efficiently, and working well together, the team was gradually drawing near us. Soon the leader would reach the ledge at −790, 460 feet above us. Their whistling, and the occasional snatches of talk that reached us, were all that we knew of the men who were deliberately risking their lives to help us save Loubens's.

The doctor took flasks, syringes and rubber tubes out of his bag and laid them out methodically on top of Loubens's body—for there was nowhere else to put them. Then he knelt beside his patient on one knee. The other he had to wedge against the rock. Labeyrie and Occhialini, in the anxious role of nurses, managed to find a firm foothold on the other side of the stretcher. Mairey handed them the flasks, and connected the pipes. He lifted Loubens's right arm, stretched it out and found a vein. The transfusion began.

Several times, during the last few hours, we had managed to laugh and make jokes; we had to do so, for Marcel's sake and our own, in order to help preserve our nervous energy. But at the moment a mood of deadly seriousness possessed us.

I put on the earphones and hooked up the throat-microphone. From now on, up above, someone was constantly on duty.

"Hello, winch! Tazieff here."

"Hello, Haroun. Janssens here. What's the news?"

Briefly I described the last few hours' work. Very soon, I told him, we were prepared to dispatch Loubens; and I asked whether they were ready for him up above.

"Yes, everything's ready. We can begin as soon as the last of the boys from Lyons has reached his post."

"Good. We'll be seeing you soon."

"Just a moment. Robert wants a word with you."

Meanwhile, the transfusion went on. Drop by drop, the colorless plasma drained out of the squat bottle, as Occhialini held it up at eye level.

"Hello. Is everything all right?"

"Yes, it's going nicely. Is there any news?"

"Tell me, did you get pictures of the accident?"

"No. Not one."

And, in fact, I had taken nothing at all. Not that the

idea had not occurred to me. Very often, during the long day, I had visualized pictures, and framed many moving scenes in my mind. Several times I had seen astonishingly photogenic subjects. But I had not touched the camera, though it had always been within my reach. Yet it was precisely to bring back as many pictures as possible that I had been sent down. Since the catastrophe, however, I had felt restrained by scruples that were stronger than my passion for reporting. Perhaps there was a touch of superstition in it: if I took no advantage of the situation, Marcel might survive.

But up above Robert was insistent.

"Perhaps you had better take some. News photographs would be a great help. Expenses are getting terrific."

I knew that he felt embarrassed.

"I see. All right. I'll take something."

I went down to the camp, where I had left the camera after my three hours' sleep. Very far away those three fitful hours seemed now.

I was glad, if that is the right word, to be alone for a few moments. By myself, I had no need to pretend that life, on the whole, was good, or that I was simply a tough robot, insensible to all that flowed around me. Moreover, I was glad to be away from the nightmarish gasping of the unconscious man.

Something sharply pulled me up. From the distance of a dozen paces, it seemed as if the force of his breathing had lessened. Or was I merely imagining things, in my fatigue?

I hardly lingered in camp. For a few seconds, I stretched myself out on the friendly elastic canvas of my bed—just long enough to convince myself that there really were good things on earth; then I picked up the camera, and set off again. I had scarcely covered 65 feet, when my only lamp went out. I shook it, squeezed it, played with the switch, screwed up the battery, but nothing happened. In total darkness, I shouted:

"Jacques!"

There was a muffled reply. Labeyrie could not have been more than 100 yards away, but the lie of the land in the cave made it impossible to hear him distinctly.

"Of course," I thought, "they can't stir from up there, because of the transfusion." For a moment I stood still in the dark.

"Let's hope I have some matches."

Luckily I had. In the flickering light of matches, climbing 100 yards was quite an athletic feat. Fortunately for me, I had had a week's experience of these boulders.

At Loubens's bedside, I took some pictures of the operation, but without using magnesium, because of the toxic gas it releases. All the lighting I had was provided by my friends' electric breast lamps, and two tiny acetylene flames. The transfusion came to an end. My companions were exhausted, after holding impossible positions for more than an hour. Mairey took the telephone.

"Hello, surface. Mairey here."

". . . ."

"Whenever you wish."

He took off the earphones. His round face looked hard, and was lined with fatigue. In silence, he considered the body of Loubens.

Time went by. What more could we do but wait? The cold, the damp and the weight of our weariness were heavy upon us. Somebody lit the stove to make coffee. The blue flames of butane gas, and the singing of the water, gave us an illusion of family comforts.

Marcel uttered a low groan, his first since he had crashed down upon the rocks. There was a second groan, and a third, and his strained gasping stopped. His furious struggle was reaching a close. There was a last faint groan, and a final exhalation of breath. Mairey bent over him, and then stood up. Motionless, and without exchanging a word, we stood looking down upon our dead friend.

Once more, the doctor bent over the body, stretched out his hand and, with his finger tips, gently closed the eyes. Labeyrie shuddered, went to the telephone and plugged in. His voice sounded sharp and frozen.

"Hello, winch! Labeyrie here."

". . . ."

"Marcel Loubens is dead."

". . . ."

"Yes. He died five minutes ago."

He disconnected and took off the earphones. I looked at my watch; it was 10:15 P.M. The catastrophe had happened thirty-six hours ago.

Labeyrie picked up the earphones again.

"Hello! We're going to have a sleep."

". . . ."

"All right. Contact tomorrow at 9 A.M."

XI

Here lies . . .

WE PACKED our bags with everything that might be useful in the camp below—the stove, the pressure cooker, a
rubber mattress, provisions and flasks. My three friends
set off over the rubble, and I went on water fatigue. The
water was still seeping out, drop by drop, from underneath the rock that had arrested Loubens's fall. His
blood was spattered about, less than a yard above the
crevice in which I was crouching, holding out the empty
tin as the water slowly collected. In spite of 4 degrees of
frost, the blood was going stale, and a sweetish aroma
had begun to fill the air. Trying to breathe only through
my mouth, I strove to put it out of my thoughts.

It was a very long half hour. But at last the flasks were
filled, and I rejoined the others in camp. Jacques and
André were boiling lentils and opening boxes of sardines.
Beppo and I dismantled the little Narvik tent, and set up
a much bigger one, in which we could all sleep, and
where we could more easily preserve some warmth. Sleep
was all we thought of, and all that we wanted. But we

had a bad night; there were too few mattresses to cover the sharp stones, and only two sleeping bags, one of them very small. It was so cold that the best we could do was to doze.

It did not take much debating, next morning, to decide that if it had been right to do everything in our power to get the injured Marcel to the top, it would be madness to risk the lives of the men slung from ledges in the shaft for the sake of a corpse. Not only was the inevitable fall of stones extremely dangerous, but the physical energies of these youngsters, and above all the quickness of their reactions, must already have been greatly reduced. Yesterday, they had performed a miracle by fixing in place 820 feet of perpendicular ladders, lowering them by the strength of their wrists alone. After they had been told of Loubens's death, they had had to climb back to the top. The last of them, we heard on the telephone, had not reached the surface till 4 A.M.

What put an end to our discussion was the irregular shape of the perpendicular shaft: that was the main obstacle to hauling up a stretcher, 6½ feet long, burdened with a body weighing 175 pounds. The only possible solution would have been by means of a winch, powerful enough to draw up both the stretcher and an able-bodied man, who could guide it over the more difficult reaches. And we did not have such a winch. Besides, we should have had to arrange for men to be posted at intervening stages, to climb up and down the ladders, disengaging the stretcher from the snags on which it might be caught—especially from the jutting limestone sheets, divided by narrow chimneys, that had been such a nuisance to us when coming down loaded with heavy kitbags. So we came to the conclusion that it would be criminal to risk the lives of our young rescuers any further. Labeyrie got into contact, and explained our point of view. His wife, Françoise, was at that moment on duty. She explained how we felt to the others, and, after a short pause, told us that they agreed.

"All right," Jacques said. "We'll ring off. Contact again this evening. But keep someone permanently on duty at the telephone. And, Françoise, on our behalf, please thank the youngsters on the rescue team, especially the boys from Lyons, and Bouillon, Bouchet and Laplace as well. For all they have done for Loubens, and for the great part they took in the struggle. *Au revoir.*"

A new day of hard work was beginning. How much easier it would have been for us to fasten the stretcher to the cable, give the signal for hauling up and then fall into the deepest of sleeps!

Mairey set off on a tour of inspection, looking for a place in the cave where Marcel could be buried.

"The best place I've found," he told us, "is in a narrow hollow, about 3 feet by 6, between two big perpendicular slabs, halfway up from the camp."

"Where is it?"

"Over there, halfway between the camp and the cable drum."

I felt exhausted, and aching all over with fatigue. What was the point in doing it this evening? We should see more clearly in the morning.

"The morning! You ass!" I thought. This must have been the tenth time I had caught myself committing this idiotic error. It seemed almost impossible to get accustomed to the fact that down here one could see no better in the daytime than at night.

The stretcher seemed very heavy as we carried it down. But we managed it without accident, one of us at the foot, and two at the head. Firmly anchored, with his back against a rock, Labeyrie paid out the rope we had fixed to the stretcher's head.

The burial took a very long time, and most of the day went by without our realizing it. We placed our friend's body in the cleft of a sort of natural grave, hollowed out between the two boulders. Marcel Loubens lay stretched

out, stiffly encased, as if in a suit of armor, in his waterproof overalls, the straps and shining buckles of his parachute harness and his strong, smooth, convex, white helmet. His left arm, still in plaster, rested beside him. His
right arm was folded across his chest. Energy had always
radiated from his features; now in death they had
acquired a noble calm, so that he looked exactly like the
effigy of a medieval knight lying on his tomb, dead but
unconquered.

Confronted with the sturdy body of our dead friend,
I was seized with a feeling of rebellion, which I could
hardly contain. Precisely a year ago, in this very cave, I
had spent an interminably anxious hour wondering what
could have happened to his adventurous spirit. So much
effort, and so much loving care on the part of his father,
his mother and his wife, had gone into the making of a
really gallant man—and then a metal pin had come
undone.

There was no earth in the cavern. The smallest stuff
we could find was a fine gravel, a few millimeters in size,
which we placed, in handfuls, on his canvas shroud. Suddenly Occhialini had a scruple of conscience: had we
done things right, and as Marcel's relatives would have
wished? By telephone we had called Casteret to ask what
their wishes might be. But who could say what were the

desires of a grieving mother and wife? Occhialini quickly clambered up to the cable, made his connection, and renewed our inquiry. He asked for Casteret, whom Marcel had looked upon as his spiritual father, and whom we knew to be almost as grief-stricken as Marcel's parents.

"Casteret, what shall we do about the ceremony? Ought we to make him a cross? Should we take off his wedding ring?"

When the canvas had been almost covered by a first layer, we started scooping up the gravel and pouring it in with our helmets. Jacques grasped a hammer and chisel, lit his pipe, and grimly began to carve an epitaph on the surface of a large slab to the left of Loubens's head.

Hours went by. After the fine gravel, we used a coarser size. Then we took stones, as big as our fists, and laid them down, first in one layer, then in a second. Gradually, we came to stones still heavier and more bulky. By now the human frame of our dead friend was completely concealed beneath a cairn of stones. The scruples we had felt faded away, and for I do not know how long we piled up great lumps of rock.

Labeyrie finished his epitaph—a cross, a name and a date, as simple and sober as the tomb itself. At the top of two huge rocks, and on a third, a little less high, we raised small cairns composed of four or five dry stones. For several hours Occhialini had been reciting in a low voice, as if to himself, poems in Spanish by, I think, García Lorca. These verses, murmured by the dead man's side, sounded like a prayer. Mairey never uttered a word, but worked like a blacksmith, manhandling 130-pound rocks. At the head of the grave he built a wall. On top, he set a block of black limestone, striped with two bands of white calc. With two squares of sheet metal, covered with white luminous paint, I fashioned a rough cross, and erected it on a sloping slab. It reflected the faintest of lights, and could be seen from the entrance to the cave, like a fiery cross shining out into the night.

All was over. We collected our lamps, ropes and helmets, and, for a moment, stood contemplating the incomparable majesty of this mausoleum. Then, worn out with fatigue, we returned to the tent.

While Jacques and André made a hot meal, Beppo took an acetylene lamp, moved its low flame up to the wall that bounded the far end of our camp terrace, and in its smoky light began to write. A quarter of an hour later, I took over from him, and finished off this inscription:

HERE

MARCEL LOUBENS

PASSED THE LAST DAYS OF HIS GALLANT LIFE

As on the night before, we slept badly. The next day, which was August 16, was entirely devoted to the ascent of Labeyrie and Occhialini. Labeyrie is a man who is as cautious as he can be daring.

"I wanted to recheck everything before coming down," he had often told us after the accident, "but I was afraid they would think I was being overcareful, and that I was frightened."

Now that his apprehensions of disaster had been proved all too well founded, he was determined to leave nothing to chance—at least, nothing that he could himself check, down at the bottom. We spent many hours binding up the gadget that fastened the harness to the snap hook, and strengthening it with brass wire. I cut our fine nylon rope into several lengths, and we fashioned a safety sling which we attached parallel to the ordinary one.

"A pity," I said. "It's a new, 10-millimeter nylon rope."

"The thing is to get out of here alive," Labeyrie replied.

Meticulously, he put on his kit, examining every hook and shackle with minute care.

"You must do the same," he told us. "Mairey, you see this cross-piece? Make sure that all of you fix it exactly like this, and that the nylon rope is arranged just so. . . . You follow?"

He picked up his small rucksack, and stowed in it a few important odds and ends that he wanted to take up with him; there was no question of weighing himself down to no purpose.

"In touch with the winch," Mairey reported.

I entrusted my Leica to Jacques, as it was temporarily out of order, and all the used films that I could find; if he came into harbor without mishap the films would be saved.

He put on the helmet he detested. It had been impossible to discover one wide enough to fit him, and this one, big though it was, pinched his head.

"Hello, surface? Are you ready? Off you go, and take it gently."

"Best of luck, Jacques."

A few minutes later I had to shut my eyes. The broad, unrecognizable shape, that was Labeyrie, was slowly rising in the dim light of our lamps, and what I saw at this moment was exactly what I had seen three days earlier in the minutes preceding Marcel's fall. And on behalf of Labeyrie slung out in space, I was terrified, more terrified than I had ever been before. Fear enveloped me in a mist that I cannot define for it was so much out of my usual experience. I kept my eyes tight shut, letting out through the hook I was holding the telephone wire that Jacques was taking up with him. Occhialini and Mairey were not so emotionally stirred. They had not witnessed Marcel's fall, and that made a big difference.

When Jacques was out of sight, my terror evaporated, and very glad I was, for fear is a most unpleasant sensation, and utterly useless. The wire was unwinding steadily, and Jacques was rising without a hitch. Two or three times he had to stop in order to move the flexible ladders out of the cable's way, in case they should get entangled with it. Thus, he was making the ascent easier for us. I watched the big spool gradually run out; we came to the last spirals and it stopped unwinding. Jacques had made his exit.

Some adjustment now had to be made to the winch, but this time we were warned about it. Besides, we were in much better spirits, now that Labeyrie was safely on top. During the days we had spent together at the bottom, I had learned to appreciate the man, and what a reliable fund of courage he possessed. I now knew that whenever Labeyrie was in charge of something, one could rest easy.

Occhialini did not leave us until about the middle of the afternoon. When I say afternoon, it is merely to place the event in time, because for us it was still night. I gave him the smaller of my two cameras; it would be one more thing salvaged if he made a safe exit. He set off very slowly, stopping often on the rubble slope in order to test the winch before he was launched into space; with all his weight, he let himself hang from the slings, doubling up his legs, and we could hear him asking on the telephone: "What's the dynamometer reading? How are the blocks behaving?"

Eventually, he was off. Pulling on the bottom wire, we tried to stop him from spinning too much. But once more I had to close my eyes. Although not so deeply moved as I had been by Labeyrie's ascent, I could feel anxiety tightening in the pit of my stomach at the sight of a living creature hanging in space, and all too gently moving upward. It was Occhialini's turn to reach the point from which Loubens had crashed down on the rocks. . . .

Occhialini's ascent took longer than the previous one. Increasing fatigue weighed down our aching shoulders.

"Will he ever get up? Heavens, how sleepy I am!"

About midnight, at last, the spool had nearly run out, and our longing for rest seemed about to be satisfied. Unfortunately, Occhialini was held up for a few minutes more on the natural ledge less than 2 yards below the exit. We did not find out the reason for this unbearable delay till two days later: it was that twenty press photographers were waiting for him, all set with flares and flashes, and he could not abide being photographed. . . .

XII

The last exploration

We had discussed the project with our friends before
they went up. In hints at first, for fear that we might
seem unfeeling. But we had proved unanimous in our
resolve. Our project was not to return to the surface until
we had resumed the exploration of the cave and, if it
could be done, discovered a passage leading still lower.
We had brooded on this ambition during the preceding
days, and gradually its realization had become a neces-
sity for us. The reason was simple. In the course of the
last few days we had gathered, through our talks with
the surface, that the world above regarded us as cast-
aways in distress, who needed above all to be rescued.
Especially now that Loubens's life could no longer be
saved, we had been reduced to mere objects of general
concern. A catastrophe had, indeed, befallen us, but if
we had asked for help, and begged for men and equipment, it had only been with the idea of bringing the injured man out of the cave in time. Now that the four of
us were the sole remaining members of the team to haul

up, the world's huge fund of pity was concentrated upon us. But it happened that none of us had a temperament that easily admitted defeat. The events and exertions of the past long week had not crushed our spirits, and we wished to prove it. In particular, we longed to penetrate into the extensions of this gigantic cavern, now that Loubens had caught a glimpse of their entrances. It was a matter of demonstrating that Loubens was right, of finding new caverns and of doing what our friend would have wanted us to do: carry on.

We had hoped to push on with our exploration as a team of four, but circumstances interfered; we had to think about the parents, friends and rescue teams on top. And so only two of us remained.

"Hello, winch! It is four o'clock, terribly late, and we're dead tired."

". . . ."

"You too! I'm not surprised. We are going to sleep. Don't expect to hear from us until 2 P.M. tomorrow."

We clambered down the familiar slope. After a flask of thick, warm extract of malt, we slid into our fleece-lined bags. It was wonderful to have a bed and hot-water bottle to oneself, with no sharp stones sticking into one's back. But it did not last long enough. Though Occhialini's traveling alarm clock was with us no more, we woke at 8:30 A.M., as we had arranged.

In circumstances like these, it is hopeless to put off getting up. That only makes the torture worse. Besides, there is the risk of falling asleep again, perhaps for hours. Without giving ourselves a chance to grumble about life, and complain against the dark, the cold, the world and humanity in general, we had leaped up, and were putting on our clothes, overalls and shoes. André started boiling some water on the butane stove. By the time that I had rummaged in our bags, and collected together the ropes, hooks, provisions, torches, lamps, camera and film that we meant to take with us, he had poured a whole tin of extract of malt into a quart of boiling water. We swallowed it, though it scorched our palates. It was so concentrated that our throats smarted, and not only because it was hot. I pulled a face, because I have never liked sweetened food.

"Go on," André said, "it'll strengthen you. And swallow this too," he added, handing me a tablet.

"Ought I to take it now? Wouldn't it be better to keep it, in case we strain our hearts?"

It was a stimulant called *lambarène*, a drug intended to induce new strength in cases of physical exhaustion.

"No. Go on. We must try to stop heart strain in advance. And we'll be taking some more at regular intervals."

"O.K., Doctor."

At 9 A.M., with our bags swaying on our shoulders, we set off for the bottom of the cave.

We made good progress; working our way round the rock we had named Gibraltar, we slipped between two boulders, wedged together in a striking conformation— at least for people passing under it—and eventually reached the edge of the shaft leading down to the Casteret cave. I uncoiled what was left of my fine orange-colored nylon rope, hooked myself on, so that André could make me fast, and slid into the narrow opening through which a fierce draft was blowing. I quickly ran down the 65-foot ladder, the lower part of which trailed over the rubble. André followed me, just as quickly. We recoiled the rope and set off briskly for the bottom, crossing the cave diagonally, in the direction of the vanishing streamlet and the gallery that had been discovered four days earlier.

Mairey was in fine spirits. He had a passion for caves and subterranean exploration. Since he had arrived at the Col Pierre Saint-Martin a fortnight ago, he had been compelled to wait and wait, until the machinery could be made to work, and consent to lower him down. Even then, there had had to be a catastrophe before he could realize his desire. And so far his stay at the bottom had been given over to anything but speleology.

Here and there in the huge darkness, where our lamps lit up only a small part of the surrounding heaps of stone, there glowed, dimly and curiously, the pale rectangles marked out by Marcel and me when we had been surveying a week ago. We crossed the cave at record speed, for our rendezvous on the telephone was for 2 P.M. And now we came to the fracture. The gallery ought to be just a little lower, and there it was! We had taken only half an hour to reach it, that was some going! At once we plunged into the opening, going down by a pebbly slope at an angle of about 30 degrees.

"Can you hear the water?"

André had stopped, and was listening.

"Yes . . . farther down. When they came back they said they had heard the river all over the place."

We went on, without meeting any serious difficulties. About 35 feet lower down we came across a small cairn, erected at the entrance to an opening that widened out to the right, and seemed to lead upward.

"This is the place they reached! And this is the opening they could not agree about."

It was here that Loubens had sensed the beginnings of a new cave, and where Labeyrie, more cautiously, had doubted his optimism. The noise of the torrent, on the left, was now very distinct. Looking about us, we discovered a narrow passage and, one after the other, entered it. There were galleries and catholes, and a cul-de-sac that obliged us to turn back and start again, but at last we came to the water. I looked at my altimeter: taking no account of the variation in atmospheric pressure, we were now at least 65 feet below the point where the stream disappeared in the Casteret cave.

"We have to take the variation into account," I said, "but I believe we are even lower down than the altimeter reading. Do you think it is the same stream?"

André had managed to descend to the edge of the water, which ran under breath-taking heaps of wedged boulders. Two yards below me, he was standing with his back against the rock, arms and legs spread out.

"Certainly," he said. "I can see fluorescine sticking to a stone over in that corner."

"So it hasn't all been washed away!"

I lay down full-length, and, leaning between the boulders, drew myself lower. It was true. The fluorescine had left a line of vermilion foam a few yards above the present water level.

"The level has gone down quite a bit in the last few days."

André tried to walk beside the riverbank, but it was hopeless. We looked for another passage. A series of cat-holes enabled us to make some progress, along a distance of 30 or 40 yards; we picked up the stream again, rumbling across the shingle, but then we came to a stop.

"We could try diving," André suggested. "If we got through this siphon, the stream might open out again afterward."

"Brrr . . ."

Some other time we might have done it. But in our present state, there was no attraction in plunging into water a few degrees above freezing point.

We had posted our way with strips torn from a piece of cloth covered with luminous paint, and this made our return journey easy. Whenever we came to a crossroad, we knew which arm to take. Back at the cairn, we edged off to the left toward a rather large opening, halfway up the rock face, some yards above our heads. Without much exertion, we reached it and, climbing over a sort of sill, entered a small cave which we rapidly crossed. There was a fresh opening, and then our lamps failed to pick out anything in the huge, dark, open spaces. I switched on the very powerful torch lent us by our chief engineer,

Pierre Louis: far off its beam of light struck a rock face. We looked at one another. Our luck was almost too good to believe. Here was a new, and certainly tremendous cave; a third cave to add to the two we knew already, reached without obstacles, and almost effortlessly.

"Haroun, what about lighting one of your flares?"

"You're right. Just a moment. I'll get the camera ready and light up."

I took the heavy motion-picture camera out of my bag. It felt very cold, and to warm it up I put it under my fleece-lined waistcoat against my shirt. Motionless, we waited, with lamps switched off. There was no sound down here, except for the occasional dripping of cold water from the vaulted roof above us. I tested the camera, and its motor was working.

"All right, André. I'm going to light up. Walk off to the right; don't look at me; and use the light of the flares to study the cave."

The fuse took a second to catch; then the dazzling light burst forth. We had arrived at the entrance to a stupendous hall, some thousand feet long. At the moment we were halfway up it, about 130 feet above the bottom, with the roof towering over us, some 120 feet high. Carefully but quickly, André was walking on the level along the right-hand wall. I followed him in the view finder.

Like a giant's, his distorted shadow was thrown up on the rugged rock face. I left him, sweeping the cave with the camera, in the hope of recording a little of its extraordinary grandeur. I reached the end of a reel, hastily inserted another, changed lenses, and began shooting again. André had vanished—at least, from my view finder. I could no longer pick out his silhouette, dwarfed and lost in this great cathedral of rock.

The flare went out, and for a few minutes I could see nothing. When my eyes were once more accustomed to the dark, and I could again use my electric torch, I stowed the camera away, heaved the bag onto my shoulder and set off on my companion's tracks. Three hundred yards farther on, he was waiting for me, his eyes sparkling with excitement.

"Haroun, this is terrific!"

We were both of us in a state of elation that can only be understood by people who have experienced the moment of discovering virgin ground. I remembered the awed feelings I had had in the Congo, when I had been the first man to tread the lava and ashes of a new volcano. I knew then that no one had been there before me, that no one previously had explored the crater, and this knowledge had intensified the curious delight with which that sinister landscape had filled me. Here, again, we knew we were the first. Neither paleolithic men, nor the potholers of today, had ever been here before us. It was intoxicating to know that we were the first human beings to survey these vaults. Vanity, perhaps, but I hope not altogether. For it is part of man's nature to be seeking always to find out and understand new things. . . .

By now we had covered about 300 yards, and we thought we had reached the extremity of the cave; then we noticed on the left that a sort of natural dam broke away from the wall and dived 40 yards downhill. Beyond this dam, the cave extended still farther.

"There must be at least another 200 yards," said Mairey, sweeping the wide new spaces with the beam of his torch.

In my bag I had a particularly powerful, 10-kilo, magnesium "bomb," which could burn for ten minutes, and which I had been keeping for some special occasion. Now, the occasion was at hand. I adjusted the camera, warmed it against my stomach, put the big flare on a rock and set a light to it.

We were astounded by the vast dimensions of the cave. Much bigger than the other two, it was 400-500 yards long by 300-400 wide, and all the more impressive because, instead of being littered with great lumps of rubble, its bottom seemed to be empty, hollowed out like the hull of a huge ship. In place of rubble, we were confronted with a panorama of rocky coagulations—slender stalactites, suspended like long wisps of straws from the majestic vaults, hanging curtains of stone, and broad, squat, dome-shaped stalagmites, looking like huge mushrooms growing on the yellowish bottom of the cave. Near by were pools of still, transparent water, in basins of fine brown clay. Taking advantage of the brilliant light, Mairey was tackling the crest of the dam. In the glow of our torches, this passage had seemed so narrow as to be impracticable. While Mairey went nimbly and carefully forward, I took shots of him. Then the mainspring jammed.

This was the last blow. With the Leica out of order and my small camera back on the surface, this apparatus was the only one left with which I could hope to bring back a documentary record, and now it was useless at precisely the moment when we were discovering wonders. In spite of all my efforts, the mainspring could not be made to work; it was jammed by nine days of cold and damp. Rummaging in my pocket, I drew out a small crank, fitted it, and started shooting by hand power; it was better to have bad pictures, even very bad ones, than none at all. I thought of a rejoinder of Michel Simon's:

"Better to have an ugly mug, than no mug at all," and my bad temper vanished.

We had just swallowed our third lambarène tablet, and the tonic effects were beginning to be noticeable. As soon as I had finished my reel of film, I shouldered my pack and set off for the narrow peak of the dam. André had disappeared. Twice I hallooed, but he was already out of earshot. I had no trouble, however, in following his trail, for it was clearly marked with luminous strips of "scotch-lite" set in prominent positions.

This is by far the best way of staking out an underground route, and I recommend it heartily to fellow speleologists. It was to a happy accident that we owed our chance of using it, and of learning to appreciate its remarkable qualities. A few days before my departure for Pierre Saint-Martin, I had been hauled up before the police on a little matter of exceeding the speed limit. When justice had been administered, the commissioner said to me:

"Would some scotch-lite be of any use to you in your caves? I have some scraps left over."

I had accepted, thinking that they might possibly come in useful, and I had brought them along rather as a last resource, for we already had a stock of metal sheets, luminously painted in the same way. As it turned out, the sheets let us down, whereas the cloth, when torn into long thin strips, proved perfect from every point of view: it was more luminous, and very much easier to stake out.

"There's a lot to be said," André remarked when we were hurrying back, without once losing our way, "there's a lot to be said for being in well with the police!"

Having skirted the crest of the dam, I came to a broad terrace of rubble on the other side of the cave; turning to the right, I followed a path that led me easily down-hill to the floor of the cavern. Looking up, I directed the beam of my torch straight to the roof, but I could not pick it out; the roof must have been at least 100 yards above me.

There was still no reply from André. In the darkness, I could see two or three luminous strips leading, 50 yards ahead, to a place where the side vaults met the ground: that was the end of the cave. Where could André have got to? Drugged with lambarène, I quickened my pace, leaping nimbly from boulder to boulder. Then I understood; though the cave came to an end, a tunnel opened at its farthest and lowest extremity. It was a black, gaping orifice, toward which the shining strips drew me on.

I entered the tunnel. Its proportions were on the same scale as those of the cave—10 yards high, and 20 to 40 in breadth. I took the time and the altimeter reading, scribbled for a moment in my damp notebook and set off briskly on Mairey's tracks. The huge tunnel ran on to the northwest, in a perfectly straight line. Half a dozen trains could have been driven through it abreast. In contrast to the sharp declivities of the three caves above, the slope had a gradient of only a few degrees. There was no water about; only heaps of boulders.

"Ho-oh!"

I was delighted to hear Mairey's call; it was good to find him again, so that we could share our vivid impressions. Two hundred yards down the tunnel, he was waiting for me. "Can you hear it?" he asked.

I had to listen very carefully in order to work out where the noise came from, for the rumbling seemed to issue from the whole rocky wall. In fact, it was coming from underneath us.

"It's the river," André said.

Parallel to it, the tunnel ran on, and we set off down it again. A little farther on, amid scattered rocks, the water suddenly appeared.

In a few steps, we had passed from a dry gallery to the banks of a big subterranean stream. This was a very much more considerable river than anything we had seen up to now; its flow was four to five times as great; it was between 5 and 10 yards in breadth, and 1 to 3 in depth.

We pressed on quickly, anxious to explore still farther, before the time at which we had to be back at the cable drum. Sometimes the path was easy, sometimes we met with awkward rocks, overhanging the crystal-clear water; twice I thought I had a good foothold, only to discover that I had dipped my foot up to the ankle in the water, not realizing that my stepping stone was underneath the surface.

After half an hour's straightforward progress down this extraordinary tunnel, we stopped at 12:45 P.M. on the edge of a wide, calm, greenish pool. Probing beyond this small lake, our lamps picked out the dark circle of the tunnel which seemed to stretch on ahead forever. I lit my last flare, and, turning the handle, shot a few feet of film. André took advantage of the light to survey the tunnel as far as he could see; he reported that it went on exactly as before.

It was a very great sacrifice for us to turn back on our tracks. We reconciled ourselves to it only because of the waiting men on the surface, who would be getting anxious about our long silence. But it was tough! According to our calculations, based on altimeter readings, we were about 2,000 feet underground, and more than a mile, as the crow flies, from the end of the cable.

We had brought off a tremendous success. For we had

really reached the base of the great limestone mountain mass, and were now at the point where, on a gently inclined plane, it rested on the underlying carboniferous schist. Almost for certain, from now onward, there would be no more shafts; only a succession of galleries leading, very likely, to the Kakouetta gorge, 3½ miles away, and another 2,000 feet lower down. What a potholer's dream it was to enter the heart of a mountain at the top, and come out again 4,000 feet lower down, having traversed the whole mountain mass within! The realization of this dream probably lay in front of us. And yet we had to turn back. Not only were we leaving off an intoxicating task of exploration; we were still confronted with the exhausting climb back to camp, and all the hazards of ascent up the perpendicular shaft.

"My heart bleeds for Marcel! He found the entrance to this wonderland, and he decided to be hauled up so that his friends would have their share of excitement."

With some tins of solid alcohol, we heated a flask of Nescafé, munched a packet of biscuits, swallowed another lambarène and turned our backs on the tempting stream of the river. We climbed back into the huge dark spaces of the cave, guided by the soft glow of our luminous strips. Reaching the big dam, we crossed its

narrow crest once more. As I felt worn out, I had to
straddle the ridge clumsily.

"Heavens! You gave me a fright," André said, watching my performance.

In this beautifully proportioned cave, we stood motionless a while, surrounded by its curious hillocks of glowing
calc.

"This cave is superb!"

"It certainly is. Let's call it after Marcel Loubens."

"Yes, of course."

All went well until we reached the Elisabeth Casteret
cave, which we crossed diagonally, heading for the flexible ladder that hung from the ceiling in the southeast
corner. I was shaping our course, since I was the one
who knew the cave; André had crossed it only once, in
the downward direction. Here there were no more strips
of scotch-lite; only some dimly luminous sheets of reddish paper, left by Loubens during his explorations a
year ago.

In spite of lambarène, I began to feel my exhaustion
acutely; I had trouble clambering over each boulder,
from which one had to drop down sharply, before starting at once on the next. Persistent cramp was attacking
the backs of my thighs; if only it did not get worse!

I do not know how it was, but we missed the exit shaft.

We had reached a high point in the cave where the vaulting curved down to join the jaggedly rocky bottom. Brought to a stop, we shone our torches, like long antennae, questingly around us. Nowhere was there a ladder; we were in unknown country. And yet, several times before I had been in this cave; in three visits, I had made six crossings, and one of them had been a detailed survey. My tired brain started to panic, and I began to wonder whether I was in my right mind. "I don't recognize this place at all. Are we really in the Elisabeth Casteret cave?"

Mairey reassured me.

"Then we must have got to the upper left-hand corner of the cave, the corner we didn't explore with Loubens. It follows that we must turn back and see what we can find to the right."

We set off again, and Mairey soon outdistanced me. I made an effort to keep up with him, but the muscles of my thighs were paralyzed with cramp. It was so painful that it doubled me up, and I lost my balance. I fell from the boulder on which I was standing, twisted my wrist and barked my skin.

"Merde!"

I could only go forward with knees bent, practically on all fours. It was laborious, and it must have looked grotesque. I felt supremely ridiculous, yet at the same

time I was filled with anxiety. Would I be able to climb
the ladder—if only I could find it?

I thought of Loubens, lost in this cave alone last year,
while I had waited at the top of the shaft for which we
were now looking. His two lamps had gone out, and he
could hear no answer to his cries. When at last we had
been reunited, he had confessed, at the end of his tether,
"I was really frightened." Now there were two of us,
and I knew, for it stood to reason, that we could not fail
to find the exit. But, all the same . . . I am still full of
admiration for the courage and self-possession that enabled our friend that time to make his way out.

A happy shout came from André: "Haroun, I've found
the exit."

I took another lambarène and, while André climbed
the ladder, massaged my legs. Within ten minutes, the
cramp had gone, and I made an easy ascent.

It was nearer 4 P.M. than 3, and we were late. Since
we had set off at 9 A.M., we had hardly paused, except
for a quarter of an hour for coffee at the farthest point
we had reached. In these six hours our exertions and
keyed-up enthusiasm had carried us far away from the
drama through which we had lived in the days immediately preceding. Its emotions once more began to weigh
upon us, as, after a final pause for rest at the top of the

shaft, we made our way up: a stale smell of blood had spread throughout the whole of the uppermost cave, and it was horrible.

We hurried to the camp. We had to be quick, if we were to spare the anxieties of the men waiting on top (they thought we were asleep); and we had to be quick, also, if we were to be hauled up before nightfall.

Nearly all our equipment had to be abandoned. We had been warned that the maximum load was 30 pounds per man and so it was a matter of selecting essentials. This meant, for me, first of all, my used films, then my expensive camera, its stand and a sleeping bag. André had nothing to carry except a few surgical instruments; in order to be less of a burden on the winch and come down as speedily as possible, he had brought no personal belongings with him, not even a change of sweater.

We divided between us the selection of goods and chattels that were to be taken up. I wrapped my camera and sleeping bag in a rubber canoe cover, left with me by Jacques, and stuffed the lot, together with the films, into a rucksack. The camera stand, and two light camp beds, belonging to Labeyrie and myself, I placed in a kitbag; within five minutes our baggage was all strapped up.

"Off we go. Are you taking the flowers?"

André picked up the cup that for the last five days had held, and miraculously preserved, the little bunch of meadow flowers brought down for Labeyrie by Occhialini. "From your wife," he had said.

Once more, and for the last time, we climbed the rubble heap, threading our way between the familiar boulders. We tried to hurry, but fatigue made our bags weigh more heavily and our muscles stiff. We reached the head of the grave. By the side of the veined black-and-white headstone, André set down the cup of flowers.

"Good-by," we murmured, and went on our way.

XIII

Four hours and a half on the end of a wire

"HELLO, winch! Mairey here."

". . . ."

"That's all right. We're putting on our kit."

". . . ."

"Very well. In half an hour. This morning we went exploring lower down, and we found a third cave; very big. Then there was a big tunnel. And quite a river, at a depth of more than 2,000 feet."

". . . ."

"You're not surprised? Well, we are! We'll be seeing you soon."

We put on our kit. It is not easy, without assistance, to get into overalls, fasten on a parachute harness, adapted in the way that we used it, and secure to the straps a haversack and a kitbag. We were both putting on our tackle at the same time, lending each other an occasional helping hand.

I made the error of not wearing my waterproof; I had left it down in the camp. I hoped to go up quickly, as

Labeyrie and Occhialini had done, without having to spend more than a quarter of an hour or so under the waterfall. I was to be proved very much mistaken.

"Well, five days ago we thought we'd have no stories to tell. Now there are all too many!"

"Yes, worse luck! . . ."

It will be remembered that before the expedition began, we had sold the serial rights of the articles we intended to write about our exploits. Now that the catastrophe had greatly increased our costs, we needed money urgently. All the more so, since we had decided to raise a small fund for Marcel's two-year-old son, Patrick Loubens. Our articles, pictures and films were going to furnish it.

I put on my helmet, fastened the cable lug to the hook and plugged into the throat-microphone.

"Hello, winch! Tazieff here! I'm ready."

"Cosyns here. How are you? We're starting to haul you up."

I turned to Mairey.

"Good-by, my friend. Let's hope it all goes well. Take care not to get cold; have something hot to drink, and often."

The cable stretched taut, and I clambered up the slope with the curiously slow gait of a man in a diving suit, when he is being hauled diagonally upward, while his weight is dragging him down. Going up by the usual route, that Loubens had followed, I reached the great boulder; after this came the perpendicular ascent.

"All right?"

"All right, thanks."

"Speak to me often," Cosyns told me, "then we shall know that the telephone is working."

Slowly I rose, a good deal more slowly than my predecessors.

"It's not going very fast," I remarked.

"Wiser, that way," Cosyns replied. "They are checking the tension on the dynamometer. You're heavier than Labeyrie."

"Of course I am; and there are all my films too!"

Looking down, which in this heavy helmet and harness called for a considerable effort, I could see the yellowish glow of Mairey's lamp. It seemed already very far off. I was spinning a little, but I was more or less kept steady by the lower telephone wire. The strong beam of my lamp swept the walls and the upper part of the rubble slope; boulders appeared and vanished again like pale ghosts.

"Talk!" Cosyns ordered. "Talk! All right?"

"Yes, yes, all right."

In spite of all the lambarène I had swallowed, I did not feel in the least talkative. On the contrary, I should have preferred to remain quite silent, adapting myself as best I could to this stupendous place, and the alarming situation I was in. Hanging some 100 feet up in space, I was being patiently drawn toward the top by a thin and almost invisible wire; surrounding me was the dark silence of the earth's center—a silence I could distinctly feel, in spite of the water drumming down on my helmet.

Then, far below me, I heard André starting to whistle the "Hymn to Joy." It had a wonderfully tonic effect. I joined in, but my whistling did not last long; the water running down my face and over my lips made it impossible. Instead, I began to sing.

"Well done!"

Through my earphones, I heard Max Cosyns's encores coming from the surface.

"Well done. Nothing could be better than the Ninth Symphony; go on, and we'll be able to check that the throat-microphone's working."

One hundred sixty-five feet; 200 feet. My lamp could no longer pick up anything in the vast gloom. Two hundred; 275 feet. Thanks to the throat-microphone, I was keeping count of my ascent. Then the cable stopped.

"Hello, what's happening?"

"A little adjustment."

A little adjustment? I was filled with misgivings.

"Adjustment of what? How long will it take?"

No reply.

"Hello. Can you hear me? How long will it take?"

Still no reply and I began to shout: "HELLO! HELLO!"

"It won't take long; it won't take long."

"But how long? Do be honest!"

"Well . . ." (I saw he was holding something back) "ten
minutes, or perhaps an hour . . ."

"An hour!" I exploded.

"We may have to let you down again."

"What!" I yelled. "What? Let me down again? But
you're mad!"

There was silence again. So I waited a moment, forc-
ing myself to be calm. Then I went on: "Hello, can you
hear me?"

"Yes."

"Look, I'm hanging in open space, and right under
the waterfall. It's absolutely the worst place for anyone
to have to wait in. Couldn't you draw me up another 50
feet, as far as the traverse at −950?"

"No, it's impossible."

I grumbled, in resignation. "Very well. All right."

The water falling on my helmet and shoulders was

gradually penetrating down my neck, in spite of the sponge cloth I had tied around it.

"What can have happened to that winch?" I wondered. "At least they might tell me."

I heard André hailing me.

"Hi, Haroun."

"André! The winch has broken down!"

Mairey asked me a question I could not catch at that distance (about 350 feet), because of the earphones covering my ears and the drumming of the water on my helmet.

I looked at my watch. A quarter of an hour had gone by.

"Hello, Max?"

"Hello?"

"Will it be a long time still?"

There was a short silence, then: "About ten minutes, if all goes well."

"Listen, I'm right under the shower, and without a waterproof. My fleece-lined waistcoat is beginning to absorb the water. Everything I'm wearing is getting heavier—I shall put on another 20 pounds. Have you considered that? It would be better to haul me up to the traverse."

"I'm sorry, it simply can't be done."

"That's too bad; well, then, let me down again."

"That can't be done, either."

"I can't go up and I can't go down," I thought. "This really is too much. What can have gone wrong with that bloody winch?"

To preserve the batteries, I switched off my lamp, and darkness engulfed me. Far off at the bottom, the glow of André's lamp served only to increase the impression of infinite space. All at once, my patience gave out:

"Hello, hello! What the devil is going on up there? I'm not a child. If it's something serious, for heaven's sake tell me! Hello!"

No reply. I waited a moment and shouted again. Still no reply. By now I was in a furious rage.

"You might at least keep in contact. Do you think it's funny down here? Hello!"

Silence.

For some minutes I stayed quiet. The water was adding terribly to my weight. I thought of those extra pounds, and of the winch that had not been strong enough to haul me up when I was dry. It was anything but a cheerful prospect. I remembered what Labeyrie had told us a week ago. While coming down he had had the task of rearranging something in the shaft. At a given moment, he had asked to be hauled up a mere 4 inches.

Not very far, in all conscience, but the answer had been: "Sorry, it can't be done." That story had left us rather pensive.

I felt far from pensive at the moment; in fact, I was mad with rage. I was yelling abuse, which was unfortunately lost on the air, since no one was at the listening post.

Limply, I hung in space, enveloped in a draft of icy air. Eventually someone spoke, and I recognized the comforting voice of Janssens.

"Hello, Haroun. How are things?"

"Terrible, Jean, terrible. What, for God's sake, is happening up there? Tell me; you know I'm no coward. Tell me what's gone wrong. And don't leave me out of contact. It's a dreadful feeling!"

"There it is, my boy. Beppo has thought of a way. They've had to take the strain off the winch; they've put some bends and hitches on the cable with telephone wire. They've made a dozen knots—everybody has turned to. And a dozen men are easing you in. Can't you feel it?"

"I can't feel anything. It seems to me that I haven't budged."

"That'll be because of the elasticity of the cable. But it's working out."

"Are there a lot of people up there?"

My anger had melted away, and I began to feel calm again.

"I'll say there are. Everyone's anxious to help—gendarmes, journalists, the boys from Mauléon, not to speak of the team. Do you know who went down first into the doline to haul on the cable, as soon as it was decided to ease it?"

"No . . ."

"Your father."

"My father? My parents are there, then?"

"Oh yes, ever since yesterday."

"They're not too worried?"

I knew my mother's nervous temperament.

"No, no. They're in good form."

"Give them my love."

Time flowed on, and so did the water. An hour passed away, and likewise the effect of the lambarène. I was overwhelmed by the weariness accumulated during nine days underground—nine days with scarcely any sleep, not enough food and too many emotions. On top of our earlier experiences, the aftermath of that last day of frantic exploring, when we had climbed and potholed for six hours, on repeated doses of lambarène, was proving altogether too much for me. Only with the drug had we been able to hold out. Now that the effects of the last tablet were wearing off, and I had no more with me, I was nothing but a miserable bundle of nervous flesh hung on the end of a wire, spinning alternately a few turns to the left and a few turns to the right. And above my head, somewhere in the dark chasm, the tap of the waterfall was eternally gushing.

I nearly broke down and wept. I began to shiver with cold, and for a while this seemed to distract me. But soon it became insupportable; in vain I tried to stop the continual chattering of my teeth. For more than three hours it went on.

From on top Janssens patiently and hopefully repeated that it would only take another ten minutes. A quarter of an hour later, and it was a further ten minutes. Another quarter of an hour, and it was ten minutes still. These "ten minutes" were what drove me to despair.

"But, Jean, please tell me frankly how much longer it will be!"

How many times I asked him that question! He put it to the men who were working at top speed on the repair of the winch.

"A quarter of an hour; perhaps twenty minutes. It all depends. Pierre Louis is drilling a hole in the axle of the block. Then it's a matter of putting in a wedging screw."

I no longer understood, but I was glad to hear these

technical details; they were, at least, something other than darkness and water, gyrations and horrible fatigue, and legs that felt nearly dead from having, at the top of the thighs, been too tightly strapped into my harness.

The wait seemed interminable, and in fact it lasted for two hours and twenty minutes. I would dearly have liked to fall asleep or lose consciousness. But that would have made things too easy. Never in my life have I felt so utterly wretched.

The kitbag episode for a moment brought me back to life. Max Cosyns asked me how many pounds of baggage I was carrying.

"About 30," I answered.

"Thirty pounds," he cried. "But 20 was the limit I told you. What have you got?"

I told him.

"Camp beds," he exploded. "But I told you to take only what was indispensable."

"Indispensable!" I muttered in revolt. "Do you think I should have come up naked?"

And I went on grumbling, "Indispensable, indeed, indispensable!"

"Let go your kitbag," he ordered.

Besides the two camp beds, which weighed 9 pounds,

the kitbag held, among other things, a first rate camera stand.

"There's the C.T.M. stand," I said. "With the rest of the stuff, there go 200,000 francs. You really want me to let go?"

There was a long pause, and then the order: "Let it go."

I unfastened the hooks and, with arms outstretched, held the precious kitbag out into the void.

"Hi, André?"

"Haroun!"

"Watch out! I'm letting the kitbag go. If you can find it, take a look at the camera stand. . . ."

"Right. Go ahead."

I relaxed my grasp, and there was a silence as if nothing had happened. It lasted several seconds—and that, on occasion, can seem a very long time. Suddenly, there was the boom of the heavy bundle, splintering on the rocks below. In a flash, I saw what a huge distance separated me from the bottom of the chasm.

My parents told me later what was happening up above. As soon as it was a question of starting the ascents, they had come up from Licq, where they had been waiting for news; and they spent several days in our im-

probable surface camp, jumbled together with the
rescuers, gendarmes, shepherds and journalists, who had
collected around the original expeditionary team. This
is how I would reconstruct events, according to the story
that was given me:

It was 5:30 P.M. Earlier, the weather had been fine,
but it was now growing overcast, and rain threatened.
From the short phrases spoken into the throat-microphone in the flat voice of Cosyns, the audience could
follow the stages of my ascent. Up to now, it had gone
without a hitch, despite my 175 pounds, and the weight
of my baggage.

"Halt!"

The winch stopped. Cosyns took off his earphones and
bent over toward the engineer. Then he had picked up
the throat-microphone, talked of adjustments, suggested
lowering me down again and, in the end, given way.

"Right. We'll try to carry out the job without sending
you down again."

Perched on the steep edge of the doline Max Cosyns,
Louis and their assistants held a whispered consultation
around the frail machine. Mme Mairey was manning
the telephone to the camp. She was heard asking them to
search among the equipment for a 5-millimeter pulley

wheel. Everyone understood what that meant. A great deal more was at stake than a slight adjustment.

The spare parts brought up did not fit, and they had to get down to repairing the winch block on site. To effect this, the cable had to be shifted a foot to one side, and raised aloft, so that the screw that had given way could be replaced. A foot may seem no distance of consequence, but there was my weight to consider, that of my bags, the friction against the rock and the strain of some 400 yards of cable. You can imagine the grip necessary to support a taut cable, 5 millimeters in diameter.

To hold the wire, while it was raised from the block, they sawed an end off the wooden stand on which the winch had been transported ten days ago, and which, luckily, was still lying around. This jury mast was inserted and embedded in the frame of the winch. In order to slip it under the cable, they had to let out some slack, and, at the same time, farther down at the entrance to the chasm, support the thin steel cable upon which, some 350 feet down in the darkness, hung the weight of a human life.

Labeyrie, Treuthard and Occhialini took on the job. Telephone wires were used as relief ropes. They were knotted to the cable, and then—heave! A dozen men bent to the task, the white metal cords biting into their shoulders.

"Hold it! Don't pull too strongly, in case it breaks!"

The teams from Pau and Mauléon were there, and with them big Bouchet, Bouillon wearing his famous hat with the hole in it, and many others. These men had hastened up to relieve the youngsters from Lyons who had left the previous evening; thinking their help was no longer needed, the men had been getting ready that morning to return home. Fortunately, they had not yet left, and for two long hours upon the strength of their arms a man's fate depended. "How's the heaving, boatmen?" Labeyrie shouted to them from the top of the winch. By instinct, he had taken command of the rescue work; with his decisiveness and quickness of eye, he combined a heartening gift for banter.

Twilight, and with it a depressing rain, gradually darkened around the little group drawn up in the rugged bottom of the doline. Climbing down the rope ladder that swayed against the cliff, my father joined them; he was followed by a hefty journalist, who could not bear being an idle witness, and came to take his part in the struggle. Like the five men up above, leaning backward behind the winch with their whole weight, all in the doline had to keep up their efforts during the entire time that the technicians took to work out and effect their difficult repair job.

In the darkness my mother was rummaging in Louis's tool bags.

"A screw, please. . . . Not that one; a 5-millimeter steel screw. There aren't any? Well, give me a metal bolt."

Someone provided a blanket; it was spread out on the muddy earth and the contents of the tool box emptied on to it. As chief engineer, Louis was sitting in front of the winch, with his back to the void, secured by an alpinist's rope. With skilled precision, he was exercising all his ingenuity, trying to carry out the suggestions of Delteil and Labeyrie. They improvised and invented the tools and parts that were needed. Louis drilled holes, cut and filed the metal and adjusted it with taps of his hammer.

Every three or four minutes—my mother had kept glancing at her wristlet watch, and wiping the rain off the glass—Cosyns replied in a tone of voice he strove to keep calm to the questions from below that everyone guessed were growing more urgent.

"I know it isn't funny for you, but safety must come first."

And he gave the order to jettison the kitbag. Then he handed the throat-microphone to Janssens, who did his utmost, in his rough, friendly way, to fight against the fatigue and anxiety of the man suspended in the pit.

"Mme. Tazieff, send him a message."

My mother was unwilling to speak herself, in case the sound of her voice would upset me.

"Tell him it's all right; tell him to be patient, and that I'm here; I bring people luck."

Never once losing their self-possession, the men at the winch worked on.

"It's done!"

All that remained was to file away three protruding millimeters. Next the log support was removed, and the wire eased back into its place on the block, carefully, so as not to spring the axle. Then the fifteen men holding up the cable could let go gently, one by one, taking infinite precautions, for a jerk might have proved fatal.

As these maneuvers had slightly put the block out of true, Labeyrie, secured by a rope, had to control by hand, with the aid of a makeshift ring, the endless winding in of the steel cable. But hope had been restored.

At last my slow ascent began again. On the edge of the doline a big fire was roaring; into it they pitched a huge stump, excavated from the earth by our young friend André Laisse. Up above, in a shepherd's hut, Morizot was cooking a reviving stew for me.

For the nth time, Janssens had said: "Just another ten minutes," and I had replied exhaustedly, "I know your ten minutes."

But it was true: the cable actually began to move.

"Good-by, André. I'm going up again. Don't get cold down there."

"*Au revoir,* Haroun. Good luck!"

For an hour and a half I was hauled up the length of the perpendicular walls, between the smooth, damp surfaces of the chasm. Here and there, I asked for a moment's rest on a traverse, and tried to get a little blood circulating in my painfully stiff limbs. Max Cosyns had taken over from Janssens on the telephone, and constantly cheered me on.

"You're getting nearer. Only so many feet . . . such and such an altitude. Good luck."

On the terrace at −262, Robert Lévi and Jimmy Théodor were anxiously waiting for me, all set to give me a hand. I arrived utterly shattered, muttered "Halt," into the telephone and flopped down on the rock, hanging from the cable like a limp sack. Jimmy called to me, but though I was more than delighted to hear his voice, I could not bring myself to utter a word in reply, or even make the slightest gesture. My body was all in. Perfectly well I could see the anxiety in my friends' eyes; and I should like to have said: "Don't worry, it's all right." But it could not be done. My brain was working, but not a nerve or a muscle would respond to it.

Later they told me they thought I had taken leave of my senses, for my efforts to speak resulted in incoherent noises, which I myself could not hear, because my ears were blocked by my helmet.

Eventually, I managed to harness my will power and make a few movements. Jimmy fed me with sugar, and I contrived to suck it and swallow. A few minutes later, and I was on my feet.

"Thanks a lot. I'm delighted to see you. It's very nice of you to climb down here to wait for me."

Under their fortnight-old beards, their friendly faces cleared.

"Go ahead," I said into the throat-microphone, "you can haul me up."

Half an hour later, I emerged on top. Night had fallen, and powerful lamps were lighting up the doline. I could not count the number of worried faces bent over the chasm. Within me a wonderful warmth of feeling possessed my breast, a feeling of brotherly love and deep gratitude to all these fellow men.

I was borne off, undressed and laid beside the fire, where the huge pine stump was flaming. My cramp-torn muscles were patiently massaged, and a meal was served me. Mother, father and friends were all around; friends I knew well, and others I had never seen before. . . .

"Listen, send the cable back to Mairey. Do it at once —it's tough waiting down there!"

Unfortunately, yet another adjustment had to be made to the winch, and André did not come up till next day. He emerged into broad daylight. . . . But his last night below he had agreed to spend alone, 1,200 feet underground—alone, with Marcel Loubens.

Set in Linotype Times New Roman
Format by Robert Cheney
Manufactured by The Haddon Craftsmen, Inc.
Published by HARPER & BROTHERS, *New York*